LES
OEVVRES DE
Mr.
MOLIERE
F.C: fe

MOLIÈRE

*d'après le tableau attribué à Pierre Mignard*

*HARRAP'S FRENCH CLASSICS*

---

# LE MISANTHROPE

By

MOLIÈRE

EDITED WITH AN INTRODUCTION
AND NOTES BY

RONALD A. WILSON M.A. Ph.D.

*University of Saint Andrews*

AND A NOTE ON FRENCH VERSIFICATION BY

R. P. L. LEDÉSERT

*Licencié-ès-Lettres Licencié en Droit*

Nelson Harrap

Thomas Nelson and Sons Ltd
Nelson House Mayfield Road
Walton-on-Thames Surrey
KT12 5PL UK

51 York Place
Edinburgh
EH1 3JD UK

Thomas Nelson (Hong Kong) Ltd
Toppan Building 10/F
22A Westlands Road
Quarry Bay Hong Kong

Thomas Nelson (Kenya) Ltd.
P.O. Box 18123
Nairobi Kenya

Distributed in Australia by

Thomas Nelson Australia
480 La Trobe Street
Melbourne Victoria 3000
and in Sydney, Brisbane, Adelaide and Perth



First published in Great Britain by Harrap Limited 1945
(under ISBN 0-245-52220-4)

Reprinted sixteen times
Eighteenth impression published by Thomas Nelson and Sons Ltd 1985

ISBN 0-17-444441-9
Print No. 02

Printed in Hong Kong

# INTRODUCTION

## 1. Molière's Background

Although Molière's life embraces two reigns, he is essentially a writer of the age of Louis XIV—an age particularly favourable to the arts. Few eras in history have produced such a galaxy of writers and artists. To know Molière is to know his age: from a careful study of his work we may learn almost as much about his time as from the accounts of historians. His plays form a vast and varied canvas, depicting the Court, the *salons*, the doctors and lawyers, the *bourgeoisie*, the family life, etc., of the day. Molière is not only a great writer of comedy, but a keen and ironic observer of life in all its varying moods, of every type and condition of man.

Before we study Molière's life and work it will be profitable to survey briefly some of the salient historical and social aspects of the epoch to which he belongs. Indeed, French literature of the seventeenth century can scarcely be studied without reference to its historical and social background, so closely are they connected.

When the fanatic, François Ravaillac, assassinated Henry IV in 1610, France was plunged into a period of uncertainty bordering on chaos, after a time of what may be termed comparative prosperity. The Queen Regent, Marie de Médicis, manifested no particular strength, either of will or character, allowing herself to be unduly influenced by foreign minions, with the result that internal strife and turmoil were inevitable. It was the Florentine, Concino Concini, who gained the Queen's complete confidence, but he was shrewd enough to approach her through his wife, Léonora Galigaï, who exerted an almost hypnotic influence over the Queen Regent. The corruption and rapacity of this pair encouraged the nobles in making outrageous demands. Indeed, the weaker the government became as a result of Concini's mismanagement, the more the pretensions of the nobles increased. Louis XIII, however, at the age of sixteen, formed a plot with his own favourite, Albert de Luynes, to have Concini killed. The Italian's murder, in 1617, was applauded by the nobles, who now hoped for greater self-aggrandizement, but de Luynes revealed himself to be as rapacious an opportunist as Concini, and as ungifted a Minister. Thanks to him, France was left in a condition of weakness and disorder seldom paralleled in her history.

To Armand du Plessis, Cardinal de Richelieu, fell the lot of restoring order in France, settling religious quarrels, and quelling dissension between the nobles and the royal power. Whatever one may think of the ruthless measures taken by Richelieu, it must be acknowledged that he strove indefatigably to restore France to her former greatness. That he was a man of singular genius is indisputable. He himself has left an interesting outline of his policy. Addressing Louis XIII, he declared :

> When your Majesty decided to accord me at once a place in your council and a great share of your confidence, I may say with truth that the Huguenots behaved as if they were no longer subjects, and that the more powerful governors of provinces acted as though they were sovereigns in the districts, the control of which had been entrusted to them. I may add that our foreign relations rested on a false basis. I promised your Majesty that I should employ all my industry and all the authority which it may please you to give me to effect the destruction of the Huguenot faction, to reduce the pride of the nobles, and to raise the prestige of France among the foreign nations to that point at which it ought to be.

Thanks to the amazing strength of his personality, he succeeded in establishing the Monarchy as a supreme power holding complete sway over the nobles, the clergy, and the political assemblies. Even the influence of the so-called *Parlement*, which was little more than a court of justice, was reduced to a minimum. One of his first master-strokes was the siege and capture of the Protestant stronghold, La Rochelle (1628), followed closely by the Peace of Alais (1629), which brought the religious war to an end. Equally relentless in his foreign policy, Richelieu was instrumental in raising France to a position of importance among the nations. It was in the midst of brilliant success that he died, in December 1642, at the age of fifty-seven.

Space does not permit of a study of how the Cardinal achieved his three main aims, which he pursued simultaneously, but it must be noted that, thanks to his intellect, skill, and iron will, he left France universally victorious: the rival house of Austria had been dealt a shattering blow, the four important provinces of Lorraine, Roussillon, Artois, and Alsace had been added to the realm, while Catalonia and Portugal had, with consummate statesmanship, been stirred up against another dangerous rival—Spain.

After Richelieu's death in 1642 Louis XIII did not change the great Cardinal's policy. He survived him only six months, however. Louis had arranged that, during the minority of the new king, affairs of State should be in the hands of a Council to be presided over by the Queen Mother, Anne of Austria. By far the most noteworthy member of this Council of Regency was Mazarin, one of four nominees proposed by Richelieu. Mazarin, who belonged to an old Sicilian family which had settled in Rome, had favourably impressed Richelieu in 1634, when sent as a papal nuncio to France. The Queen, who was more than a little attracted by him, gave him complete control over the administration of the country. Although a friend and admirer of Richelieu, and imbued with the Cardinal's ideas, Mazarin was altogether a man of a much more ordinary calibre.

Not long after Mazarin's rise to power a number of overweening nobles, nicknamed the *Cabale des Importants*, clamouring to undo Richelieu's work, rushed to Court, hoping to gain new favours and privileges ; but a plot to murder Mazarin being discovered, they were quickly relegated to their estates, or, as in the case of the Duke of Beaufort, to prison. Anne and Mazarin soon found themselves faced by energetic resistance, not only on the part of the nobles, but also of *Parlement* and people. Reform of taxation was the main demand of the two latter, while the nobles sought to restore their former power, of which Richelieu had deprived them. On the death of Louis XIII France had been left in a state of acute financial embarrassment, which Mazarin's maladministration and personal greed considerably aggravated. Taxes were so great, and in most cases so unjust, that in 1646 there were no fewer than 23,000 persons in prison ; and it is chiefly this period of financial crisis which gave rise to the long and bitter struggles called the *Fronde*. It is impossible here to follow the development and phases of the *Fronde*. It must suffice to note that its repercussions were felt throughout the whole of France.

A reconciliation was effected between *parlement* and Court in 1648—the year of the Treaty of Westphalia and the close of the Thirty Years War. The nobles, however, continued their own self-interested struggle for power, but, in the end, thanks to Mazarin's diplomacy, the Court won the day. Nothing had been gained by the conflict. The people were more sorely oppressed than ever, the nobles found themselves more or less powerless, while the *parlement* was entirely deprived of its previous political significance.

Louis XIV's reign, like so many other long reigns, presents two clearly defined aspects: a period of brilliance and prosperity, and a period of decadence and misfortune. The most scintillating phase of his reign is that which extends from the death of Mazarin, in 1661, to the death of Colbert, in 1683. In every sphere great men distinguish this epoch of Louis' reign. In charge of internal administration there was the outstanding Minister, Colbert. War was in the hands of Turenne, Condé, Duquesne, and Louvois. In the realm of art Lebrun, Claude Lorrain, Poussin, Mansart, and Perrault are but a few distinguished names; the literary world has an illustrious array to show —Molière, Boileau, Bossuet, Bourdaloue, La Fontaine, Madame de Sévigné, and Racine. From 1683, however, there is a perceptible waning of this glory until Louis' death in 1715.

In 1661, at the age of twenty-three, Louis assumed absolute rights in the government of the country. He it was who chose Ministers for the main offices of State. He it was who held the power to dismiss them, if such were his pleasure. Louis sincerely believed that he was the "earthly representative of God," and that his power here below should be supreme. Bossuet went so far as to establish his divine right from specially selected passages in the Bible. All the *parlements* were subjected to the king's will. In 1667 he issued an edict ordering the registration of all royal decrees within seven days. In the event of any resistance Louis attended the session himself, and saw to it that the edict was duly passed. The *parlement*, then, was little better than the king's mouthpiece. Of the so-called "three estates," the nobles and clergy were deprived of practically all political power. It was on the middle class that Louis bestowed certain privileges.

He found the members of this particular section of his subjects more amenable to his demands, better educated, and more loyal than the others. Moreover, being the descendants of a class long crushed beneath a feudal yoke, they did not, as yet, realize the iniquities of absolute monarchy. Knowing that he held them in the palm of his hand, Louis appointed them to the main administrative offices.

In the provinces there were *parlements* very similar in function to the Paris Assembly, but their powers were even more restricted. In the sixteenth century governors had been appointed in the provinces, their duty being to represent the king loyally. These governors, who were members of the nobility, gradually assumed great personal power, rendering themselves practically independent in their provinces. They even regarded their positions as hereditary. Aware of the lengths to which they might go if unchecked, Richelieu had advised Louis XIII to appoint *intendants* to whom the governors would be answerable. These officials were thus placed in full charge of justice, police, and finance, and it was their duty to supervise the nobles and the local *parlements*. In the end the governors became merely nominal representatives of their provinces. In the reign of Louis XIV the *intendants* represented the absolute power of the monarchy in a fashion previously unknown. Each presided over a *généralité*, and, in this way, the whole territory of the provinces was brought directly under the king's control.

The importance of the Court reached its zenith in the reign of Louis XIV. Under Louis XIII Versailles had been merely a royal hunting-box, but Louis XIV created on the estate a palace befitting a monarch who held absolute sway over his realm. His servants at Versailles numbered roughly four thousand. Of this multitude many were nobles of the highest rank and distinction, who were pleased to be lords of the bedchamber, grooms, and gentlemen of the king. The most trivial of the king's activities was accompanied by what now seems unbelievably elaborate ceremony. Courtiers removed their hats when crossing his empty room, and bowed deeply before the cupboard containing his linen, as if before an altar.

Let us consider briefly some of the aspects of the ceremony attached to Louis' daily life. He got up at eight o'clock, whereupon courtiers appeared in his room in groups of descending importance. This ceremonial was called *les entrées*. For the *lever*, or rising, there were six *entrées*, at the end of which about a hundred courtiers stood in the royal bedchamber. Only nobles of the highest rank were privileged to be present when the king left his bed (*petit lever*) and put on his dressing-gown. Those of the least exalted rank arrived only when he had washed and finished dressing. It would seem that the monarch's morning ablutions were of a most perfunctory nature—he merely rubbed his hands on a towel saturated with toilet spirits. (It is interesting to note that Louis XIV is said to have taken but one hot bath in his life, and that only on his doctor's orders.) With regard to his dressing, it was likewise the occasion for much formal ceremony, his shirt, for example, being presented to him in a covering of white silk by a prince of the blood. There was a definite ruling as to who should hold each arm of the garment. And thus various ceremonies accompanying the king's activities proceeded throughout the day. Whether he dined, walked, or hunted, an elaborate ritual was considered to be essential. At the end of the day his bed-going was accompanied by as much complicated ceremony as the *lever*. Only the very highest nobles were permitted to witness the last stages of the *coucher*, as the procedure was called. Louis was thus considered something of a deity, his satellites scarcely daring to believe him subject to the same natural laws as the rest of mankind.

That Molière held, on the whole, an unfavourable opinion of many courtiers of his time is obvious from the pungent and witty pen-portraits which he gives of them in his plays. We shall see later that access to the Court permitted him to come into contact with personages who find most lifelike counterparts in his comedies. Careful study of *Le Misanthrope*, for example, reveals that Alceste may be identified with Molière, who was enabled to pronounce judgment in his play on noble personages whose conduct and opinions he had studied closely in real life. Reproaching the fickle Célimène with her attachment to a foppish *petit marquis*, Clitandre (Act II, Scene 1), he gives an admirable portrait of what appears to have been a type frequently encountered at Court. Sarcastically he speaks of " l'ongle long qu'il porte au petit doigt . . . sa perruque blonde . . . ses grands canons . . . l'amas de ses rubans . . . sa vaste rhingrave . . . sa façon de rire et son ton de fausset," and he chides Célimène for being attracted by such meaningless outward trappings. Acaste, another fatuous *marquis*, the bosom companion of Clitandre, shows himself to be an effeminate, conceited creature whose main concern would seem to be his appearance :

> Je suis assez adroit ; j'ai bon air, bonne mine,
> Les dents belles surtout, et la taille fort fine.
>
> (Act III, Scene 1)

Act II, Scene 4, of *Le Misanthrope* is of some importance in a study of Molière's attitude to certain nobles. The reception at Célimène's is almost the seventeenth-century equivalent of a modern afternoon party in high society. The unpleasant and trivial gossip reveals a lack of sincerity which Molière later describes as *une vertu rare au siècle d'aujourd'hui*. To judge by the uncomplimentary accounts which these high-born people give of their friends behind their backs, we are led to form the conclusion that their circle was composed, for the most part, of conceited bores and fools. Molière, in this important scene, is able to express his own opinion of types with whom he has come in contact. He speaks of the nobleman who, in his own words, " trouve toujours l'art de ne vous rien dire avec de grands discours," of Géralde who speaks of no one but dukes, princes, and princesses ("le nom de monsieur est chez lui hors d'usage"), of Bélise, whose conversation consists only of commonplaces, of Cléon, who is popular merely because he has a good cook and entertains well. Clitandre and Acaste appear to have little more to do than to while away their time listening to trivial gossip. To be back at Court in time for the *petit coucher* is their only important responsibility.

The historian Duruy goes so far as to state that Louis XIV, mindful of past troubles with the nobles, deliberately " attempted to encourage in them a taste for frivolity, which, in most instances, became a taste for disreputable pleasures. . . . They were compelled to spend in idleness or in debauchery the talents from which the country might have profited." While there is certainly much truth in Duruy's statement, it would be erroneous to conclude that there were no serious-minded nobles at Court. Even the Acastes and the Clitandres prided themselves on being conversant with the latest books and plays, while the Court was graced by some eminent men and women of letters endowed with considerable literary talent.

In Molière's day the Court played an influential role in the world of art and letters. The success of any writer might well depend on the favour of the king and his circle. As we shall later see, Molière was destined to be particularly favoured by Louis XIV and his *entourage*. Molière's father was, for many years, in the king's service as *valet de chambre tapissier du roi*, one of whose duties was to assist in the making of the royal bed, and Molière himself is said to have served at one time in a similar capacity.

Whatever may have been the political and social iniquities of the reign of Louis XIV, there is no doubt that he revealed himself as a beneficent influence in the literary world. Particularly from 1660 onward did he bestow special favours on writers and artists. He took directly under his protection those writers who, up till then, had been patronized by individual noblemen. In 1663 he drew up a *feuille des pensions*, on which the names of all the greater writers of the day were to be found. Under his patronage various academies were founded—*L'Académie des inscriptions* in 1663, *L'Académie des sciences* in 1666, while *L'Académie de sculpture et de peinture* was reorganized in 1664. Louis XIV manifested personal interest in these and other institutions, thereby elevating men of art, science, and letters to a position of importance and dignity which they had never previously occupied, unless they were of noble birth.

Louis XIV invited to his court the great writers and artists of the day, treating them as the equals of the noblemen who surrounded him. There is no doubt that he respected deeply artistic and intellectual prowess. To those possessed of such talent he was by no means an arrogant sovereign. Indeed, as in the case of Molière, he protected them against the criticism and jealousy of his own courtiers. It is noteworthy that Louis was seldom mistaken in those whom he selected for special favour or distinction. He chose Bossuet as his son's tutor, and Fénelon as his grandson's. Bossuet was also entrusted with the composition of the official funeral orations (*oraisons funèbres*). It is significant to record that when

Boileau informed the King that, of all the poets of the time, Molière was undoubtedly the greatest, the monarch is said to have replied "Je ne le croyais pas; *mais vous vous y connaissez mieux que moi.*" Such a remark speaks eloquently for his profound respect for great men of letters.

Second only to the influence of the King in literary affairs was that of the *salons*. Of these, by far the most famous and influential was the so-called *hôtel de Rambouillet*, founded by Catherine de Vivonne, daughter of a French ambassador at Rome, and wife of the Marquis de Rambouillet. From 1608 to 1660 the *marquise* received in her celebrated *salon* the most distinguished members of society and the greatest writers of the time. Refinement in manners and purity of language appear to have been the chief aims of the *salon*—dangerous aims, since they were later to degenerate into the exaggerated affectation or *préciosité* so often ridiculed by Molière.

Madame de Rambouillet's *salon* was the ideal meeting-place for men and women of letters who wished to discuss new poems and plays or hear first readings of new literary productions. The activities of the *hôtel de Rambouillet* have been conveniently divided into three periods. The first, from its inception in 1608 to 1630, one may term a brilliant period of preparation. Among the principal guests at this time were Richelieu, still Bishop of Luçon, the Cardinal de la Valette, and the Princesse de Montmorency. Madame de Rambouillet's eldest daughter, Julie d'Angennes, assisted her mother in entertaining the visitors to the *chambre bleue*, where the receptions were held. Some men of letters, frequently protégés of noblemen, or themselves of noble birth, were admitted to the *salon*. Of these Malherbe, Conrart, Vaugelas, and Voiture are noteworthy. Des Granges has shown how three distinct literary influences sought, during this first period, to secure pride of place in the *hôtel*—that of

Malherbe, of Honoré d'Urfé, and of the Cavalier Marin; that is, respectively: sincerity and purity of style and language, freed from all foreign influence, especially that of the ancients; the double influence of the Spanish and the Italian *roman pastoral*, of which d'Urfé's *L'Astrée* is the most important French contribution; finally, the excessively refined and precious *italianisme* of Marini's pastorals.

From 1630 till about 1645 Madame de Rambouillet's *salon* entered a new and brilliant phase of development. During this period the most important guests were La Rochefoucauld, the duc de Montausier, who was later to marry Julie d'Angennes, Mlle de Bourbon (the future duchesse de Longueville), and the romantic novelist Mlle de Scudéry, who later founded a *salon* of her own. Writers were much more numerous than during the earlier years. Georges de Scudéry, Rotrou, and Scarron were among their number. Corneille visited the *salon*, where he read his *Polyeucte* to the guests. It was there that the young Bossuet preached one of his first sermons. Not all the activities of the *salon* were serious, however. Country excursions and picnics, masked balls, impromptu entertainments, and other *divertissements* were indulged in, especially by the younger members. It was in 1641 that the duc de Montausier presented Julie with the famous collection of madrigals named *La Guirlande de Julie*, each of which, accompanied by a flower design, represented one of his beloved's virtues.

Julie's marriage in 1645, the death of the marquis de Rambouillet in 1653, and the general uneasiness caused by the *Fronde*, were among the main causes of the decline of the *hôtel de Rambouillet*. Indeed, Arthénice (an anagram of Catherine invented by Malherbe), as her friends called the *marquise*, died in seclusion in 1665. During this latter period some truly brilliant women had frequented the *salon*, among them the talented Madame de Sévigné and Madame de La Fayette, both of them women of extreme intelligence and sensibility. Along with them should be mentioned Henriette d'Angleterre (duchesse d'Orléans) and Madame de Caylus. But, while the previous generation had interested themselves primarily in polemical topics, such as the political and theological questions discussed in the *salon*, these new recruits indulged to a greater extent in subjects more essentially feminine, writing in a delightful, intimate fashion and showing in their conversation that *esprit* which is always associated with their names.

In all, the *hôtel de Rambouillet* was a most valuable institution for the fostering of literary taste and appreciation along with the other graces essential to people of quality. It is not surprising, then, that the *marquise* was copied by others who sought to set the tone in the literary and social world. Unfortunately, under less judicious guidance than that of Madame de Rambouillet, the *salon* was to become preoccupied with much that was superficial and trivial. While, with regard to language, the aim of the *hôtel de Rambouillet* was the intelligent and justifiable one of "tout dire sans brutalité comme sans obscurité," it seems that the rival *salons* in Paris, and particularly those in the provinces, spent much of their time inventing absurd circumlocutions for everyday objects. Somaize's *Grand Dictionnaire des précieuses* (1660–61) gives many amusing examples of the length to which the *précieuses* went in their affectation: teeth, for example, were no longer referred to as *les dents*, but as *l'ameublement de la bouche*, while a candle was honoured by the epithet *le supplément du soleil*. It is little wonder that Molière, always an ironic observer of human foibles, wrote his *Précieuses ridicules* (1659), in which he ridiculed the *habituées* of the more superficial *salons*. Molière had closely observed some particularly affected *précieuses de campagne* during his travels with his theatrical company, and it is they who provided him, in large measure, with material for his play. It is interesting to note that Madame de Rambouillet applauded the play cordially, realizing, of course, that Molière wished to reprove those who aped the really valuable *salons* such as her own, and who misrepresented their aims and teachings.

It must not be thought that literary activity and the appreciation of literature were the sole prerogative of Court and society circles. The part played by the *bourgeoisie* should not be forgotten. Education became more widespread among the middle classes as the century progressed. While many of the nobles became impoverished in the service of the king, members of the *bourgeoisie* amassed considerable fortunes, which enabled them to provide their sons with the very best of school and university education. Whether as business men, magistrates, or men of letters, these citizens formed an important part of the French reading and theatre-going public. Authors bore their tastes in mind when writing books or plays, knowing that they were often more learned and critical than the readers and spectators of nobler birth.

Himself of the bourgeois class, Molière is on his own ground when depicting the typical family life of his age and holding up to ridicule many of the types with which he came into contact—the social climber, the miser, the hypochondriac, etc. In this province he is a past master. To know plays such as *L'Avare*, *Le Malade imaginaire*, and *Le Bourgeois gentilhomme* is to know much about life in Molière's own time. *L'Avare*, for example, provides us with some interesting sidelights on bourgeois family life in the seventeenth century. The miser, Harpagon, belongs to the richer *bourgeoisie*, which, aping the nobles, deemed it essential to employ the services of cooks, coachmen, stewards, and other *valets*. The bourgeois, copying the nobles, lived in a house with an interior court and garden, and such is the setting of *L'Avare*. We can see also, from this play, how great was the authority of a father over his sons and daughters. If the State suffered from centralized administration, so did the family. With regard to marriage, the father had almost complete control over his children's destinies, enjoying the power to force a union likely to prove to material and financial advantage, irrespective of the wishes of his offspring. A daughter who opposed her father's will concerning matrimony almost invariably ended her days in a convent, while a son guilty of similar independence was liable to imprisonment or corporal punishment. The *dot* was all-powerful, personal affection being of secondary importance.

Of the professional classes with whom he was familiar, it is the medical profession, above all, that Molière chooses to ridicule and castigate in his plays. What infuriates Molière more than anything else is the charlatanism, combined with the pomposity, pedantry, and ignorance of the average medical man of the time. It is in *Le Malade imaginaire* (1673) that Molière most eloquently satirizes the medical profession, but *Le Médecin malgré lui* (1666) and *L'Amour médecin* (1665) likewise provide him with excellent opportunities of lashing out at the medical quacks and charlatans who had failed to cure his own illnesses. In his day doctors, for the most part, were a prey to every manner of superstition, while medical science seems to have developed but little since medieval times. Lectures on medicine were still delivered in Latin, while practical anatomy was almost non-existent. Most ailments were treated in the same way, namely by the purging, blood-letting, etc., which afforded Molière material for many farcical scenes. It must be stated, however, in all fairness, that medical science made considerable progress during the last years of the century.

In pouring out his scorn on the medical profession Molière is faithful to the tradition of medieval satirical writers and Italian farce. But behind his ridicule of the doctors' absurd costume, their playing on the credulity of their patients, and their blind mistrust of new ideas, there is an important philosophical idea, namely, the belief that the work of nature, essentially beneficent and good, is frustrated by the practice of medicine. Béralde's speech in *Le Malade imaginaire* (Act III, Scene 3) fittingly sums up Molière's own convictions: "La nature, d'elle-même, quand nous la laissons faire, se tire doucement du désordre où elle est tombée. C'est notre inquiétude, c'est notre impatience qui gâte tout, et presque tous les hommes meurent de leurs remèdes, et non pas de leurs maladies."

Although it was not until 1778, long after his death, that *L'Académie française* honoured Molière, it should be noted that the Academy was founded during Molière's lifetime. It was, in many ways, simply an elevated type of *salon*, which found its origins in literary meetings at the house of a man of letters to whom we have already referred—Valentin Conrart. Cardinal Richelieu himself was largely responsible for its organization as an official body in 1634, while, in the following year, the king granted letters patent. The University protested against this new assembly of men of letters, whose competition it feared, but now the Academy was firmly established. The immediate work, stipulated by Richelieu, was to produce a dictionary, along with grammatical and other treatises, with a view to purifying and embellishing the French language. The dictionary was eventually completed in 1694, but the rest of this Herculean task has been only partially accomplished.

## 2. Molière's Life and Work

The above brief sketch of Molière's background may help to throw some light on the century in which he was born. Molière was not the dramatist's real name, but one which he assumed. His father was named Jean Poquelin, his mother Marie Cressé, and it was in January 1622 that Jean-Baptiste Poquelin was born in Paris. His father, who carried on a successful upholstery business at the Halles, was, in 1631, appointed *valet de chambre tapissier ordinaire du roi.* His mother he lost when only ten. It is fortunate that Molière was brought up in a typical Parisian bourgeois environment, for it afforded him much invaluable material for the plays which he was to write. It is unlikely that he enjoyed a very happy childhood, since he lost his mother at such an early age, while his father, according to some accounts, was vain and avaricious. It has been suggested that we may attribute to this Molière's portrayal, in certain plays, of proud, unloving mothers, while some critics have found an echo of his father in Harpagon and M. Jourdain. Nevertheless, his father provided him with an excellent education at the Jesuit *Collège de Clermont*, where, it is said, he met the prince de Conti, who later became his patron. The fact that the sons of nobles and of tradesmen attended the same college points to the liberal nature of the institution. It is thought that the instruction given him at the *Collège* by the epicurean philosopher Gassendi left a very deep impression on the mind of the boy.

It was the desire of Molière's father that his son should study law on concluding his course at the *Collège de Clermont*. The facts regarding Jean-Baptiste's legal studies are somewhat obscure. He may have pursued them at Orléans, but, as it was possible to have a degree conferred on payment of a certain sum, irrespective of the candidate's merit, it has been suggested that Molière's father procured a licentiate of law for him in this fashion. It is clear, however, from some of his plays, that Molière did possess detailed legal knowledge.

In this same year, 1642, it seems that Molière accompanied Louis XIII as *valet de chambre tapissier* to Narbonne —his father would have liked him to follow him in his profession, but Molière's heart was neither in upholstering nor in pleading at the bar. For long he had been fascinated by the stage. Early visits to the *hôtel de Bourgogne*, where, with his maternal grandfather, he had witnessed stirring theatrical performances, had made a deep impression on his mind. The theatre, then, was to be his future career.

In 1643 he claimed an inheritance and along with a certain Béjart family and some other friends founded *L'Illustre Théâtre*. It was at this time that Jean-Baptiste Poquelin assumed the stage-name of Molière. For two years (1643–44) the troupe attempted to gain a public, but they seem to have been ill-fated from the very outset. Paris, faithful to the *hôtel de Bourgogne* and the *Théâtre du Marais*, had no time for any other theatrical venture. And so August 1645 saw Molière imprisoned for debt in the Châtelet. Hope was not dead, however, for, on his release, he decided that fortune would smile on the troupe if they made a tour of the provinces.

From 1645 to 1658 Molière and his company travelled through the provinces of France. To begin with, they joined forces with the troupe of Charles du Fresne, but this collaboration was terminated about 1650. Careful research has provided us with fairly reliable information regarding Molière's travels with *L'Illustre Théâtre*. In 1647 the troupe played at Toulouse, Albi, and Carcassonne; in 1648 at Nantes; in 1649 once more at Toulouse and Narbonne; in 1650 at Agen and Pézenas. In 1652

Molière established his headquarters at Lyons, from where the company made several theatrical tours to Vienne, Dijon, Avignon, Grenoble, and Bordeaux. But Lyons was always the centre to which they returned. It should be recorded that such was the fame of *L'Illustre Théâtre*, that it was called upon to provide entertainment for the States of Languedoc (a sort of provincial parliamentary session). It was in 1653, during a season at Pézenas, that Molière came across his old school friend, the prince de Conti. Delighted with the troupe, the prince made them visit Montpellier in 1653, 1654, and 1655, and Pézenas once more in 1655 and 1657.

Information concerning the repertory of *L'Illustre Théâtre* is, unfortunately, scanty. It contained, no doubt, a large number of both serious and comic plays by the authors of the day. We do know that Molière presented Corneille's *Nicomède* at Bordeaux, while it is almost certain that the works of minor dramatists, such as Rotrou and Thomas Corneille, were included. Familiarity with the work of contemporary dramatists was bound to be of great importance in the development of Molière's own dramatic writing. Amongst his earliest works are farces such as *La Jalousie du Barbouillé* and *Le Médecin volant*, a *genre* in which he excelled, but it was not till 1655 that Molière presented, in Lyons, his first great comedy, *L'Étourdi*, to be followed in 1656 by *Le Dépit amoureux*. Both of these plays are inspired by the works of Italian writers.

One cannot stress too much the importance of these years spent in the provinces in the evolution of Molière's dramatic art. Here he had ever before his eyes a veritable kaleidoscope of types and manners which Paris alone could never have offered him. Indeed, without his experience in the provinces we should, no doubt, have lost many of his most brilliant studies.

Finally, in the year 1658, Molière decided to try his luck

in Paris once more, and, after a short season at Rouen, returned to the capital. With him he brought the two comedies we have mentioned, and a large number of farces which had charmed provincial audiences. It was on October 24, 1658, that the company first played before the Court at the Louvre. Such was the success of the entertainment that the king granted Molière permission to use the *Salle du Petit Bourbon*, while his brother bestowed his favour on him, allowing the company henceforth to be known as the *Troupe de Monsieur*. It was in the *Salle du Petit Bourbon* that Molière presented in November 1659 *Les Précieuses ridicules*. The following year the king's architect decided to demolish the *Petit Bourbon*, whereupon Molière feared that his wanderings might begin anew. Monsieur, however, allowed him to use the *Salle du Palais-Royal*, which Richelieu had had constructed, and it was there that Molière presented his great works till the end of his days.

Though at first suspended for a fortnight, *Les Précieuses ridicules* was a brilliant success. La Grange, who was secretary and treasurer to the company, has recorded its extraordinary popularity. We may state that the production of this play marks the beginning of Molière's career as a writer of comedy. No longer did he depend on traditional Italian farce for his inspiration. Instead, he had found it in a section of French society whose affectation and deplorable lack of taste cried aloud, in his opinion, to be satirized on the stage. It is said that a voice from the pit encouraged him with the words: "Courage, Molière, voilà la bonne comédie!"

From now until the end of his life Molière gave to the world that galaxy of comedies and farces which have secured for him a place among the great dramatists of all time. In the year following the production of *Les Précieuses ridicules* Molière presented *Sganarelle*, in which he reverts to the stock-in-trade of traditional farce. His next play, *Don Garcie de Navarre, ou le Prince jaloux* (1661), in which jealousy is presented in a tragic light, he termed a "*comédie héroïque*," but it met with little success. *L'École des maris* (1661), on the other hand, was a great success, as was also *Les Fâcheux*, produced in the same year. The year 1662 marks the appearance of Molière's first *grand ouvrage*, *L'École des femmes*. It is impossible here to discuss the play in detail, but it is sufficient to say that the work gave rise to polemical discussions as important as those associated with *Le Cid* and *Andromaque*. *La Critique de l'École des femmes* (1663) and *L'Impromptu de Versailles* (1663) are short replies to his many bitter and, at times, jealous critics.

Certain critics have regretted the fact that Molière was obliged to expend so much of his time and genius on the writing of Court plays and ballets. Such *divertissements* include *Mélicerte*, *Les Amants magnifiques*, *Le Mariage forcé*, *La Princesse d'Élide*, and *Le Sicilien*. While it is to be deplored that Molière dissipated so much of his talent on the hasty production of minor comedies, ballets, and farces, it must not be forgotten that access to the Court allowed him to gain, at first hand, a wealth of material which he was able to use in his brilliant satires of the *petits marquis* as of the *grands seigneurs* of the time, nor should it be forgotten that it was under the King's protection that Molière was able to ridicule the nobility, their outward trappings and manners, and castigate their vices on the stage. His time, therefore, was not as ill-spent as many critics would have us believe.

In 1664 Molière did, however, present before the Court a play of a deeper nature than his *divertissements*. This was *Tartuffe*, which depicts a vice as heinous as Harpagon's avarice—religious hypocrisy cloaked in a mantle of piety. Public presentation was forbidden until August 5, 1667, but on the following day the play was suppressed by parliamentary action. It was not until 1669 that *Tartuffe* was permitted on the Paris stage, and even then only in a modified form. In 1665 appeared Molière's first five-act work in prose—*Don Juan*. This play, which belongs to the category of *comédie de mœurs et de caractères*, afforded Molière the opportunity of chastising moral depravity, hypocrisy, and other vices. As with *Tartuffe*, Molière's enemies were scandalized by many scenes in *Don Juan*, and the author was, once more, obliged to make certain alterations.

It may be that Molière felt that his attempts at incorporating profoundly polemical subjects in his comedies had borne but little fruit, for henceforth, while not abandoning his pungent satire and criticism, he restricted his attacks to subjects less dangerous than religion and morals.

*L'Amour médecin*, produced in 1665, is one of the first plays in which Molière pours his scorn on the doctors of his time. It is an elaboration of his early farce *Le Médecin volant*, which, as we have seen, he composed during his tour of the provinces. In *Le Médecin malgré lui*, produced in the following year, Molière once more ridiculed the medical profession. The same year saw the curtain rise on *Le Misanthrope*, which Faguet, in his critical study *En lisant Molière*, has called " le chef-d'œuvre de la délicatesse, de la finesse, de l'esprit . . . et en même temps de la psychologie juste et profonde." 1668 marks the appearance of three more plays : *Amphitryon*, an adaptation of a comedy by Plautus, *George Dandin*, a farce, and the masterpiece *L'Avare*, which, like *Le Misanthrope*, allowed Molière to expose another of mankind's moral sores—avarice. In *Monsieur de Pourceaugnac* (1669) Molière's reminiscences of provincial French life are more vivid and satirical than in any other of the plays. The provincials are likewise ridiculed in *La Comtesse d'Escarbagnas*, which did not appear until later (1672). More important than either of these is *Le Bourgeois gentilhomme* (1670), in which Molière takes to task another type representative of a section of society—the snobbish bourgeois. In the following year *Psyché, tragédie-ballet*, was produced in collaboration with Corneille, Lulli, and Quinault, while in *Les Fourberies de Scapin* Molière reverts to early farce. In 1672 Molière was able to make a final pronouncement on the pedants whom he had early satirized in *Les Précieuses ridicules*: *Les Femmes savantes* is nowadays considered to be one of his great masterpieces. And in 1673 Molière rounded off his cycle of satirical comedies with *Le Malade imaginaire*, which allowed him to make a final thrust at the medical profession. It was while playing the part of Argan in this play, on February 17, 1673, that Molière was taken ill. He had never been of robust health, and had overtaxed his strength with the combined responsibilities of author, actor, and manager. He was taken to his home in the *rue de Richelieu*, where he died shortly after the performance. In Molière's time actors could not be buried in consecrated ground, and he was no exception. It was only after imploring the king himself that his widow was able to have him buried by night in a Christian grave.

Molière's life had been one of incessant activity. As manager of *L'Illustre Théâtre*, writer, and actor, he seldom had a moment's respite. During his period of greatest activity (1658–73) he wrote no less than twenty plays. There is no doubt that he amassed a considerable fortune and was able to enjoy many comforts; he had much to make him happy, but he was inclined to be morose: "il fit rire, mais il ne riait pas." This pessimistic strain in his character was caused no doubt by ill-health. Yet he was a kind, generous, and lovable man, always ready to be of service to his friends. When advised not to appear at that ill-fated performance of *Le Malade imaginaire* his one thought was for those who would be unemployed if he failed to act.

### 3. (A).—Comedy before Molière

In view of Molière's debt to his predecessors, it will be necessary, before we examine his own art, to consider briefly the general features of comedy before his time. The study of medieval and renaissance drama is too vast a canvas to permit here of anything but cursory treatment. A review of the main features of comedy during these periods will, however, enable us to assess to what degree Molière is indebted to those who went before him. If we study the dramas of the twelfth and thirteenth centuries in France we are most forcibly struck by the strange mixture of serious and comic elements in the plays: for example, in Jean Bodel's drama *Le Jeu de Saint-Nicolas* (probably beginning of thirteenth century), we find, side by side with lofty themes of deep religious significance, comic interludes depicting, somewhat irrelevantly, the contemporary life of the time. It may be safely stated that these comic interludes contain the germ of comedy as Molière was to conceive it many decades later.

Adam de la Halle is an important name in a study of French comedy before Molière, or, indeed, in a survey of the development of the *genre* up to modern times. Before Adam de la Halle, who, like Jean Bodel, belonged to Arras, no comedy, pure and simple, had existed. As we have indicated, religious plays contained comic scenes for the amusement of the spectators, but it is the *Jeu de la Feuillée* (probably *circa* 1262) which has the distinction of inaugurating the *genre* of comedy proper. The fact that the play is entirely comic and secular is of considerable importance in our study of landmarks in the evolution of French comedy. The construction of the comedy is clumsy, while its action is impeded by the introduction of purely fictitious characters who have no connexion with the other players. The *Jeu Adam*, as the play is also called, since it contains so much of the author's family history, has been described as " un assez singulier mélange de comédie satirique, aux vives personnalités—et de féerie." A reference to an *avare* is worth recording, since it points to many subsequent portraits of misers in French comedy. Adam, having asked for money with which to go and study in Paris, is refused all financial assistance by his father, who declares himself to be very ill. The doctor comments: " C'est d'un mal que je connais bien ; on le nomme avarice."

The fourteenth century runs its course without the appearance of any French comedy. Nevertheless, the miracle plays of this time, though of an essentially religious character, could not dispense with the comic element. In the midst of serious scenes from the Old and New Testaments a comic interlude, frequently improvised, was introduced, especially if the audience showed signs of boredom or any perceptible lack of interest. It must be admitted that the farcical elements were often more popular than the main religious theme, and it is not surprising, then, to find the farce proper assuming a separate existence and even superseding the miracle plays, which were eventually forbidden by law in 1548. In these early farces we may discover much that will find an echo in Molière's comedies. They were intensely amusing, almost invariably vulgar, and generally naive. It is interesting to note, especially as we wish to establish some bond between them and Molière's comedies, that they often contained satirical references to the clergy, the militia, the law, etc., of the time. It was in much the same way that Molière was to satirize contemporary life and customs on the stage.

Another type of play worthy of mention here is the *sotie*,

which, although a morality play, contained certain comic elements. The *sotie* was a popular medium for pungent caricature of contemporary events and institutions. Only when references became too obvious or likely to arouse feelings of discontent were representations forbidden by law. Louis XII showed himself to be an indulgent patron of the *sotie*, and it was during his reign that this *genre* enjoyed its greatest success and popularity. Francis I, on the other hand, would tolerate no political references and stipulated that the *sotie* be restricted to satirizing aspects of contemporary life of a purely general nature.

The *sotie* was performed by the *Enfants-sans-souci* or *sots*, whose leader was the so-called *Prince des Sots*. The performers, who were probably impecunious students or care-free strolling players, were dressed in jesters' costumes of green and yellow. Perhaps the most famous *sotie* on record is Gringoire's *Le Jeu du prince des sots* (1512), which is full of references to the quarrels of Louis XII and Pope Julius II.

In the fifteenth century we also note the important development of the farce, which, as we saw, had begun to seek a separate existence from the miracle plays in the previous century. The farce came much nearer to the *véritable comédie* than either the miracle play or the *sotie*, since it contained far fewer allegorical characters and political allusions than these *genres*. It was, on a small scale and within its limits, the true comedy of intrigue and manners (*comédie d'intrigue et de mœurs*). Even though its plot and setting may be based on traditional tales and folklore, shrewd observation of types and customs gives it a new lease of life. The most famous farce of the fifteenth century is *Pathelin* (1470), the author of which is unknown. Whoever may have written it, one fact is clear—the author of this, the first comic masterpiece in French literature, was a real artist. The construction is masterly; the exposition is clear and concise, the various incidents are well-knit and follow one another in logical sequence, while the *dénouement* is carefully worked out. The characters of merchant, lawyer, shepherd, and judge are true to life, each speaking a tongue befitting his state. The judgment scene, in which they are all assembled, has been called "un chef-d'œuvre de justesse et de variété." With regard to language and style, the author, whether he be the celebrated Villon or some less illustrious writer, has succeeded in writing French at once so natural and spontaneous that critics have declared that nothing more precise or unaffected exists in comedy before Molière.

With the Renaissance we note distinct developments in comedy. While in essence it remains a combination of fifteenth-century farce and the morality play, it gains in polish and depth by virtue of the influence of Plautus, Terence, and Aristophanes, whose works make a particular appeal to the writers of the time. Ronsard, A. de Baïf, and others translated various works of these great writers of antiquity.

The influence of Italian comedy was, however, by far the most important for sixteenth-century writers in France. It was felicitous in that it taught French writers of comedy to vary their situations and plots, but less happy in that it introduced a plethora of conventional stock characters such as old men (frequently misers), tutors, valets, rather colourless lovers, etc., whose speech and behaviour were stereotyped to a degree.

Jodelle's comedy in verse, *Eugène* (1552), which was considered as something of an innovation, is an amusing satire on the contemporary clergy. Remy Belleau's *La Reconnue* and Jacques Grévin's *La Trésorière* (1558), both comedies in verse, also enjoyed a certain popularity, but Pierre de Larivey's comedies in prose are by far the most important contributions to sixteenth-century comedy.

Larivey (1540–1611), who was of Italian parentage, became a canon of the church of Saint-Étienne at Troyes. Coming from a family of printers in Venice, he had a detailed knowledge of Italian comedy, and his plays are either imitations or translations of Italian writers. His procedure was to follow his Italian model fairly closely, but to make such modifications in setting and speech as were necessary in order to make his plays truly French. In this way he grafted what was best in Italian comedy on to contemporary French comedy without spoiling the essential merits of either. Of his comedies, *Les Esprits* (1579) is perhaps the best known. The play is an adaptation of Lorenzino de Medici's *L'Aridosio*, while Terence and Plautus also supply the author with important material. In *Les Esprits*, as in Larivey's other comedies, there is but little attempt at character delineation. His works are comedies of intrigue in which the development of the plot is the author's main preoccupation. It is important to note that Larivey is one of Molière's most important precursors, and that *Les Esprits* was one of the principal sources for *L'Avare*.

Towards the end of the century comedy in verse reappears without contributing anything noteworthy. Minor authors become more and more Italian in the worst sense, flooding the stage with time-worn situations and stock characters. Indeed, it is not till Corneille presents his first play *Mélite*, in 1629, that true comedy reappears. At the time of its appearance comedy was, for the most part, mere buffoonery and ribaldry. In his *examen* of the play Corneille himself speaks of the reasons for its success: "La nouveauté de ce genre de comédie . . . et le style naïf qui faisait une peinture de la conversation des honnêtes gens furent sans doute la cause de ce bonheur surprenant." So great is Corneille's renown as a writer of tragedy, that it is frequently forgotten that he made his literary *début* as a writer of comedy. His *Le Menteur* (1643) is one of the principal comedy classics of French literature. It has been said—with what accuracy we cannot state—that Molière declared: "Sans *Le Menteur*, j'aurais sans doute fait quelques pièces d'intrigue, mais peut-être n'aurais jamais fait *Le Misanthrope*." Be this as it may—possibly the statement is an invention of Corneille's admirers—it is significant that, between the appearance of *Le Menteur* and Molière's first plays, there is little worthy of note in the field of French comedy. One may then conclude that Corneille is a true forerunner of Molière.

There are, of course, isolated examples of comedy before and after *Le Menteur* which show sufficient merit to be mentioned briefly here. Desmarets de Saint-Sorlin (1595–1676) is noteworthy, especially as his satirical comedy *Les Visionnaires* (1637) provided Molière with certain traits of character for Bélise in *Les Femmes savantes*. Boisrobert (1592–1662) deserves mention on account of *La Belle Plaideuse* (1654), in which one finds shrewd observation of contemporary society—a pleasant change from the extravagant situations borrowed from Spanish and Italian plays which figured so largely in the comedy of the time. It should be noted that Molière is indebted to Boisrobert for certain scenes in *L'Avare*. Cyrano de Bergerac (1619–55) must also be mentioned, *en passant*, since his *Pédant joué* (1654) provided Molière with the famous *scène de la galère* in *Les Fourberies de Scapin*. Of greater note is Quinault (1635–88), whose charming comedy in verse, *La Mère coquette* (1665), was long a favourite with French audiences. This play contains certain scenes which, most likely, furnished Molière with material for *L'Avare*. In conclusion, reference should be made to Scarron (1610–60), who occupies a place apart in the history of seventeenth-century French comedy. He is best known for his burlesque comedies, *Jodelet* (1645) and *Don Japhet d'Arménie* (1653), but he also devoted himself to other literary *genres*. The keynote of all his writing is its burlesque character, which sacrifices verisimilitude to the wildest extravagance of situation and characterization. The raciness, frivolity, and fantasy of his plays assured them of considerable success, and they occupied, accordingly, an important place in the French theatrical repertoire of the seventeenth century.

### 3. (B).—The Art of Molière

Our brief sketch of comedy before Molière will help us to make some assessment of the extent of Molière's debt to his predecessors. Even as far back as the fourteenth century we note types in the farces of the time which are strangely reminiscent of some of Molière's characters; in the *sotie* we meet satire which can well be compared with Molière's; and, later, Italian comedy reveals how much he was indebted to this *genre* for his plots and general use of action and intrigue. In his essay on the progress of French comedy, Professor Saintsbury has made some interesting remarks on Molière's debt to, and connexion with, his predecessors. Rather than emphasize Molière's actual indebtedness, however, the writer has pointed out that a likeness is sure to exist " whenever men of any age or country allow themselves to be guided by nature." Comedy of all nations and languages is after all very much the same, he declares. A comparison of great tragedies of different ages such as *Prometheus*, *Othello*, *Cinna*, and *Octavia* reveals differences before all else, but " what principally strikes him [the reader] in reading *The Birds*, *As You Like It*, *Les Précieuses ridicules*, the *Mostellaria*, are resemblances. Here, at least, there is some proof that man is really, and not merely in scholastic imagination, a ' laughing animal.' "

It is, of course, obvious, as we have indicated, that Molière owes much to his forerunners with regard to dramatic structure and general types. Yet any debt must seem small in comparison with all he did for French comedy. One critic, commenting on Molière's originality, has written : " The parts may belong to others, but the whole is his own." Let us turn, then, to this " whole " and note wherein lies the true greatness of Molière's art.

Molière is much more than a writer of comedy : he is, in addition, a philosopher and moralist, a keen observer of human foibles, a merciless critic of men. And yet his avowed aim in comedy was simply to please—to please both court and pit. In his *Critique de l'École des femmes*, Molière writes on the subject : " Je voudrais bien savoir si la grande règle de toutes les règles n'est pas de plaire, et si une pièce de théâtre qui a attrapé son but n'a pas suivi un bon chemin," and again, " Je dis bien que le grand art est de plaire." But how was such an aim to be achieved ? How was he to reconcile the taste of Versailles with that of the *Halles* ? He tells us himself—once more in the *Critique de l'École des femmes* : " . . . lorsque vous peignez les hommes, il faut *peindre d'après nature*. On veut que ces portraits ressemblent, et vous n'avez rien fait si vous n'y faites reconnaître les gens de votre siècle . . . c'est une étrange entreprise que celle de faire rire les honnêtes gens." It is in this fidelity to nature that Professor Saintsbury sees the keynote of Molière's greatness. In his excellent essay, from which we have already quoted, he has written : " . . . it was in teaching his brethren, the French comedy dramatists, to give themselves up to the guidance of nature more thoroughly than they had dared to do, and in raising the drama from the position of copying mere humours and stock subjects, that Molière achieved his greatest success."

Since Molière " paints after nature," he takes life in its

infinite variety of moods, with its numberless types, as his canvas. Everywhere he went he studied carefully those whom he met, listened attentively to the conversation of nobles and commoners. On account of this deep preoccupation with human nature his friends called him *Le Contemplateur*. Indeed, what strikes us most in Molière's great characters is their truth to life, even though, at times, he has tended to caricature certain of their traits. Molière's success in portraying true-to-life types is largely to be explained by the fact that he places his principal characters in a series of situations which allow us to study their every aspect. We see Harpagon, for example, as the head of a family, as usurer, miser, and doting lover. Molière reveals Alceste's misanthropic nature in the light of Philinte's faithful friendship and gentler philosophy, or in contrast to Célimène's coquetry. His procedure has been felicitously compared with that of a chemist who subjects a body to a series of experiments in order to note its different reactions. Molière always took good care to place his characters in the *milieu* most likely to reveal them to the best advantage. It is a significant fact that the greater part of his comedies have bourgeois family life as a background—a fact not to be wondered at, since Molière here was on ground with which he was specially familiar.

Molière's almost psychological preoccupation with every aspect of his characters made inevitable the creation of types as complex and enigmatic as in real life. "Il peint d'après nature." Now nature, life, or whatever one cares to call it, is, in essence, rather sad than gay. It is not surprising, then, that there is hardly a comedy by Molière, whether it be *L'Avare*, *Le Misanthrope*, or *Les Femmes savantes*, which does not contain the makings of a tragedy. How can one depict a father such as Harpagon, detested by his children, spreading gloom and misery all around him, or a worthy man such as Alceste, the plaything of a coquette, without coming perilously close to tragedy? Nor does Molière seek to avoid the serious or tragic issues in his comedies. He does not, however, linger long over scenes of a tragic nature, but, by some happy comic or even farcical *coup de théâtre*, ingeniously takes our minds from the tragic scene which he had wittingly introduced. It must be remembered, too, that Molière always had a predilection for tragic roles, and it is interesting to note that perhaps the most famous portrait of him by Mignard represents him as Cæsar in *La Mort de Pompée*.

Much has been written about the moral, or, in the opinion of Bossuet, Fénelon, and Jean-Jacques Rousseau, the immoral teaching of Molière's comedies. It would be absurd to try to demonstrate that Molière's works are consciously didactic. We have seen that his primary aims were to please and to be true to nature. Both of these aims would have been defeated had he attempted to make the stage a pulpit in accordance with his critics' desires. Comedy, in Molière's eyes, can be truly moral only by being true to nature, and truth to nature can never be achieved by disguising the weaknesses of virtuous characters, or by concealing the good points of their more wayward fellow-men. Molière has shown, however, that, on the whole, those who yield to vice, passion, pride, and vanity sooner or later fall victim to their ravages, and that those who resist their influence have at least inner satisfaction, if not always outward success. Even so, Molière's critics have accused him of ridiculing the authority of fathers and husbands. But, to take a single example from *L'Avare*, he never intended to justify Cléante's unfilial behaviour. He simply wished to show the pernicious effects of Harpagon's avarice on those nearest to him—that one vice is punished by another. And this example may be multiplied in the other plays.

We have referred more than once during this study to truth to nature, and a final word should be said on what Molière meant by 'nature.' His statement that he "painted after nature" has given rise to still further criticism. It is rational and disciplined nature that Molière extols, not primitive instincts and absolute liberty. He always studies man in relation to his environment, and insists on his moral obligations to his fellow-men.

Like other aspects of Molière's work, his style has often been criticized. It was La Bruyère who somewhat pungently remarked: "Il n'a manqué à Molière que d'éviter le jargon et le barbarisme et d'écrire purement." It is, of course, easily understood that a purist such as La Bruyère is shocked by the inequalities of Molière's style, but, in making the statement just quoted, he shows how completely he, like so many of his fellow-writers, failed to see what is truly great in Molière's writing. It is true that many of Molière's plays were hastily written, and that, at times, he neglected the niceties of what is known as style, but he never neglected to make his characters speak naturally. Every character, whether noble or bourgeois, speaks the language which he would use in real life. We may almost say that there are in Molière's plays as many styles as there are different characters. Molière in no wise set himself up as a stylist. His aim in writing was truth to life and naturalness, and his characters speak accordingly. He is, in this respect, comparable with Shakespeare.

In levelling his accusation against Molière's style La Bruyère no doubt had in mind Molière's characters belonging to the peasant and servant class, whose language was certainly not designed to conform with academic standards of literary elegance. But La Bruyère's very criticism is tantamount to praise, for it shows how completely Molière succeeded in reproducing the speech of real types. Molière himself, who had been absent from Paris during the language-refining process of the *salons*, had retained a full-blooded, vigorous, and blunt manner of speaking. His stay in the provinces made it possible for him to amass at first hand the invaluable material for peasant types such as Alain and Georgette in *L'École des femmes*, Lucas and Jacqueline in *Le Médecin malgré lui*, or the amusing Charlotte and Pierrot in *Don Juan*. As a realist Molière was obliged to make these characters speak the incorrect, rough tongue which they would have employed in real life. What if they repeated themselves, or joined phrase after phrase with the conjunction *et* which appears to have shocked the critic Schérer so profoundly? After all, as Lanson has pointed out, the language of Molière is primarily intended for the ears, not the eyes, and the critics have made a vast blunder in judging comedies so rich in natural verve and spontaneity as if they were books. No! La Bruyère, Fénelon, Vauvenargues, and Schérer stepped on dangerous ground when they attacked Molière's style. Had he, for example, made his peasants speak after the manner of d'Urfé's conventional village types, he would have failed utterly as a realist and as a writer of true comedy. Like his great English predecessor, Shakespeare, Molière found his style in the mouths of prince and peasant alike, and therein lies, in large measure, the true greatness of his art.

## 4. Le Misanthrope : The Play

*Le Misanthrope* has been called " la pièce des connaisseurs " in Molière's writings, and, indeed, discriminating critics throughout the world have accorded this work a place apart among his comedies. Faguet calls it " le chef-d'œuvre de la délicatesse, de la finesse, de l'esprit, du ton de bonne compagnie, et en même temps de la psychologie juste et profonde." Voltaire did not hesitate to write :

"L'Europe regarde cet ouvrage comme le chef-d'œuvre du haut comique," while Goethe, in one of his conversations with Eckermann, declared that he read *Le Misanthrope* over and over again, and that to him it was one of the most precious works in the world. Boileau, likewise, held the play in very high esteem; and yet, when the comedy was first produced at the Palais-Royal on June 4, 1666, it was not received with any degree of enthusiasm and would doubtless have been withdrawn, had not Molière subsequently added *Le Médecin malgré lui* as a bait for the less discriminating members of the public. Nevertheless, with the intermittent support of *Le Médecin malgré lui*, *Le Misanthrope* was performed about thirty-four times in 1666. We may therefore conclude that, although the play was not a popular success that appealed to the average theatre-goer of the time, it did eventually establish itself and gain the admiration of most of the people whose opinion Molière really valued.

Various explanations have been put forward for the mediocre success of *Le Misanthrope*. The Court mourning on account of the death of Anne of Austria has been given as an important factor. The support of the king was thus denied Molière, and, as we know, royal patronage played an important role in literary success in the seventeenth century. Grimarest, however, gave perhaps the simplest and most likely explanation when he wrote: "Pour vingt personnes qui sont susceptibles de sentir des traits délicats et élevés, il y en a cent qui les rebutent sans les connaître. . . . On n'aimait point tout ce sérieux qui est répandu dans cette pièce." *Tout ce sérieux*—therein lies the true explanation. The public, used to farcical situations and hilarious action, could make little of a comedy which to them simply was not one. Profound thought, analysis of character, pungent satire of contemporary characteristics and customs, almost entirely unrelieved by farce, certainly did not conform to their conception of comedy.

Lack of action and an insufficiently involved plot also provided grounds for dissatisfaction with the play as far as the general public was concerned; and it must be admitted that there is a certain justification for this criticism. Action would appear to be more basically essential to a successful comedy than philosophy. Yet what is the action of the first act? Alceste loves a young widow, Célimène, whose coquettish disposition distresses him—and that is all. The second is little better: Alceste wishes Célimène once and for all to decide between her many admirers and himself. The third act, from the standpoint of plot, is almost entirely devoid of action: the prude, Arsinoé, who is jealous of Célimène, offers to prove to Alceste, on whom she herself has designs, that his beloved does not love him. The fourth and fifth acts show a little development of what plot there is, but, even at the end of the play, the action is not brought to a really decisive conclusion.

It is true that Molière in his greater works showed little interest in the mere mechanism of the plot, but in *Le Misanthrope* the treatment is unusually desultory, intrigue and action being reduced to a minimum. Some incidents are not explained—*e.g.*, Arsinoé's possession of Célimène's letter, and certain aspects of the affair with Oronte—while others such as the lawsuits and the Dubois scene, have little bearing on the plot. Alceste's love for Célimène alone may be said to form a dramatic framework for the play, and even this is by no means a substantial foundation.

What critics of the construction of *Le Misanthrope* fail to take into account is the fact that the greatest art frequently utilizes restricted means of expression. This deliberate classical economy of means is particularly noteworthy in *Le Misanthrope*.

The French classical dramatists insisted on the observance of the unities: the play must be restricted to one place, and the action to a single day; but in *Le Misanthrope*, Molière, going a step farther, reduces the action to a few hours and confines it within the limits of a single room. Strict economy is used even in the number of characters who, with three unimportant exceptions, belong to the same social *milieu*. Here are no crowds of motley persons as in Shakespeare, no *bons bourgeois* and buffoons as in Molière's other comedies. Prejudicial as it may be to dramatic action, this economy in characters and setting allows Molière the better to reveal the real action which is concentrated in the minds and hearts of the characters rather than in their actions.

It is not hard, then, to understand that those who sought animated action and intrigue in *Le Misanthrope* were destined to disappointment. Similarly, those intent on finding farcical situations and boisterous comedy were more than a little dismayed. Even in *Tartuffe* there had been an abundance of comedy, not to mention farce, which formed a skilful and pleasing contrast to the serious and dramatic elements in the play. But here there is no Dorine, no Madame Pernelle, no Monsieur Loyal. Indeed, there is only one farcical scene in the play—Act IV, Scene 4. The comic character, Dubois, is skilfully introduced in a manner typical of Molière, for in the preceding scene comedy was bordering on tragedy. With an odd mixture of tenderness, melancholy, and fury, Alceste has been chiding the fickle Célimène and reproaching her bitterly with her behaviour, when, suddenly, the pendulum swings from serious drama to light-hearted comedy with the appearance of the comic fellow, Dubois. It is worth drawing attention to the fact that Molière frequently uses this *procédé* to save the situation when his comedy approaches too near to tragedy.

While there is no doubt that the action of the play and construction of the plot leave much room for improvement, it is not suggested that those who took exception to the lack of farcical comedy should have been gratified by the interpolation of further scenes such as that in which Dubois appears. Molière skilfully calculated the amount of 'low' comedy he might safely introduce without jeopardizing the texture and pattern of his masterpiece.

Molière may have 'played to the gallery' in previous plays, but in *Le Misanthrope* he wished to appeal to those capable of appreciating what Voltaire called "*le haut comique*" in his appreciation of the play. What is this higher comedy as opposed to the farcical Dubois scene? One might say that it is true comedy, less coarse and artificial than the conventional medieval farcical situations —comedy which makes us smile rather than laugh uproariously, or, as Donneau de Visé has aptly put it, which makes the spectator *rire dans l'âme*. It results, in large measure, from the paradoxical situations in which Alceste finds himself: that of the sincere man in love with a capricious coquette; the blunt, outspoken moralist in a worldly, sophisticated setting; the contrast between Alceste's rather ponderous seriousness and sincerity, and the fatuity of the *marquis*. It arises from the excesses caused by his righteous wrath, his invectives, his tirades, and from the striking contrast between him and the indulgent, easy-going Philinte. It is interesting to note at this point that whole speeches which Alceste delivers were based on Molière's earlier work, *Don Garcie de Navarre*, which had not been printed when *Le Misanthrope* appeared. Molière delved deeply into his earlier play in order to put the tirades of his jealous prince into the mouth of Alceste. Indeed, *Don Garcie* has been fittingly called *Le Misanthrope avant le Misanthrope*.[1]

[1] Doumic has dealt at some length with this aspect of the play in his study of *Le Misanthrope*.

The characters of *Le Misanthrope* have been the subject of varied and conflicting studies. In the case of Alceste many critics have spent a considerable amount of time drawing analogies between the hero of the comedy and people from real life. While such researches are interesting and in some measure profitable, it strikes us that they are not of primary importance in a study of Alceste. It is of course useful to know that by virtue of certain characteristics Alceste resembles the duc de Montausier, while others suggest rather Boileau and Molière himself. But it is doubtful whether Alceste, a truly great creation of Molière's mind, can be thus restricted, no matter what analogies are to be found between him and contemporary personages. Alceste is in truth himself—the child of Molière's fertile imagination and creative powers. We agree with Doumic when he writes: "C'est un des exemplaires d'humanité dont aucun original ne peut se vanter d'avoir fourni le modèle, et à qui ressemblent par la suite des milliers d'êtres vivants qu'on jurerait s'être modelés sur eux."

Can one trace the cause or causes of Alceste's misanthropic nature? Frequently, prolonged disappointments in life produce misanthropy, but we are told of none in Alceste's life. He is a rich, successful young man with most of the things which normally render life agreeable; but just as Molière makes his miser a rich man, so he presents Alceste as a man endowed with much to make him happy. His misanthropy—if misanthropy it is—is not due to any external circumstances but to some inward peculiarity of his nature. He seems to have been born morose and serious, with a relentless predisposition to discover what is faulty in both people and things. Does this mean that he is small-minded and ungenerous in his words and deeds? On the contrary, he aims so high, entertains such an exalted ideal of human conduct, that he is unceasingly shocked and infuriated by mankind—but, let us repeat, this is a reflexion not of a cantankerous disposition, but of an inexorable desire to help his fellow-men to improve themselves. Faguet goes so far as to say that Molière neither depicted nor wanted to depict a misanthropist. As he says, the misanthropist hates, despises, and avoids his fellow-men, whereas Alceste wishes to reform them, which indicates some degree of devotion to them. Faguet's comparison between Alceste and Philinte is interesting and worth summarizing at this point. Molière presents us with two characters who know the failings of men; one (Alceste) is still at the stage of railing against their delinquencies, while the other (Philinte) contemplates them with resignation and a touch of sarcasm—two misanthropists, perhaps, if one uses the term in a very broad sense. Alceste, says Faguet, is what Philinte was four or five years previously; Philinte is "*un Alceste assagi.*"

It has been objected that a man with Alceste's ideas would not easily succumb to the charms of a woman such as Célimène, but the truth of Alceste's remark, "Mais la raison n'est pas ce qui règle l'amour" (Act I, Scene 1), is obvious. He loves a coquette, he is furious with his own weakness, but just because he pursues truth and sincerity passionately, he does not attempt to conceal his love for Célimène. This frankness is a highly commendable trait in Alceste's nature, and reveals him as a truly human character.

We have seen that much of the gentle humour of the play is due to the situations in which Alceste finds himself. Largely on account of Célimène he is discovered out of his element in the fashionable *salon*, expressing himself with a bluntness unheard of in such a *milieu*. He, therefore, appears at times to be a somewhat ridiculous figure; but then it would not be in keeping with Molière's aim to paint true-to-life portraits if he did not show Alceste's foibles. He is proud, he is irascible, and by reason of these failings frequently ridiculous, despite his intrinsic integrity. That Molière wishes to present Alceste as a highly esteemed rather than a ridiculous character is shown, however, by the fact that he is well-liked by almost every one in the play, Philinte, Célimène, Éliante, and Arsinoé. Molière has proved, to quote Faguet, that "le vertueux est un peu insupportable, un peu raillé aussi, mais plus ou moins secrètement aimé de tous."

It would be difficult to discuss the character of Philinte without reference to Alceste. They are even in some respects almost complementary, and some critics have maintained that they reveal different aspects of Molière's own personality. We have already referred to Faguet's perspicacious comparison of Alceste and Philinte, and noted certain points which indicate a resemblance, and others which point to differences, in character and disposition. Far from being a mere foil to Alceste, Philinte is an individual, showing complexities of character just as much as Alceste. There may even be grounds for affirming that he, rather than Alceste, is *le misanthrope* for, inwardly, is he not perhaps more disillusioned with his fellow-men than is his friend? Having passed through a period of Alceste's storm and stress, he has now become resigned to the ideas and conduct of those who surround him, without necessarily approving of them. Perhaps the main lesson which Molière wishes to teach, by means of Philinte, is that, if we would live happily in human society, we must needs show patience and sympathy in our contacts with our fellow-men. Alceste, on the other hand, would appear to represent the other side of the medal, and, through him, Molière would wish to emphasize that, in our dealings with society, we must at all costs be true to our principles and ideals.

An interesting repercussion of Alceste's uncompromising nature is Philinte's occasionally exaggerated complaisance—*e.g.*, his unnecessary praise of Oronte's sonnet, his tolerance of Célimène's slanderous remarks. It would seem that, the more Alceste rails and censures, the more Philinte becomes indulgent and tolerant. This trait is eminently true to life and reveals in Molière a striking grasp of human psychology.

Molière's portrait of *Le Misanthrope* and his friend Philinte became the subject of heated controversial writing and discussion. Contemporary and subsequent critics and writers of repute wrote at considerable length of the play in general, but of Alceste and Philinte in particular. Fabre d'Églantine in his *Le Philinte de Molière* (1790) went so far as to present a sequel to *Le Misanthrope*, in which Alceste and Philinte, modelled on Rousseau's ideas, are revealed respectively as the personification of virtue and vice.

In Molière's own time Fénelon had reproached him with having given in his play "un tour gracieux au vice, avec une austérité ridicule et odieuse à la vertu"—an accusation which was further developed with considerable skill by Jean-Jacques Rousseau in his *Lettre à d'Alembert sur les spectacles*. Despite a certain justification for some of his statements, Rousseau is mistaken concerning Molière's basic motives in *Le Misanthrope*. His misinterpretation of Molière's portrait of Alceste may be judged from the following quotation: "Vous ne sauriez me nier deux choses: l'une qu'Alceste, dans cette pièce, est un homme droit, sincère, estimable, un véritable homme de bien; l'autre que l'auteur lui donne un personnage ridicule. C'en est assez, ce me semble, pour rendre Molière inexcusable. . . ." Rousseau refers to Alceste's qualities of integrity and sincerity, and deplores the fact that Molière makes him appear ridiculous, but what he fails to distinguish is the true nature of the ridiculous side of Alceste's character. Had Molière made the ridiculous aspects of Alceste's nature encroach on and vilify his integrity, Rousseau's censure could have been applied to Molière with full justification. But Rousseau failed to see that Alceste's sterling qualities remain intact, and that his ridiculous characteristics are the logical outcome of these qualities, and finally that Molière would not have painted a true portrait had he shown him to be wholly virtuous—in short, an ideal character.

Of Philinte Rousseau writes : " Ce Philinte est le sage de la pièce : un de ces honnêtes gens du grand monde dont les maximes ressemblent beaucoup à celles des fripons . . . qui, de leur maison bien fermée, verraient voler, piller, égorger, massacrer tout le genre humain, sans se plaindre. . . ." This judgment is manifestly distorted and exaggerated. Far from being " le sage de la pièce " Philinte is purely and simply an accomplished and experienced man of the world, endowed with the qualities and failings which such a term implies. He is certainly neither the rogue nor the egoist suggested by Rousseau's remarks. Rousseau's great mistake lies in his seizing upon certain superficial and external manifestations in Philinte's disposition without taking the trouble to analyse them and find out whence they come. In any case, Molière probably underlined some of Philinte's foibles, certainly not to present him as " le sage de la pièce," but to show the dangers of excessive indulgence and tolerance.

To complete the portrait of Alceste, Molière shows him in love with Célimène. Molière's study of this attractive, coquettish young woman is one of the high-lights of the play, and reveals deep insight into feminine psychology. Much speculation has been made as to who supplied the original inspiration for the character of Célimène, and various ladies, from Molière's own wife, Armande Béjart, to famous figures in contemporary French society, have been mentioned. While such investigation is interesting, it is not essential to a study of Molière's Célimène. Molière, no doubt, borrowed various traits in the composition of this character from the high-born ladies whom he met at Court. Above all, Célimène is a *grande dame* of the age of Louis XIV : indeed, her scintillating social life is as important to her as her flirtations. In fact, one is often tempted to think that to shine in her *salon* is the *raison d'être* of her whole existence. "Moi, renoncer au monde avant que de vieillir," she exclaims with horrified dismay when Alceste suggests that they withdraw together from the artificiality of Court life. This declaration is particularly revealing in judging Célimène's character. For her nothing exists outside her own aristocratic circle. No ordinary men of letters are admitted to her *salon* as they were to Madame de Rambouillet's. Moreover, it would appear that Célimène is not specially interested in the arts. If they are essential for her own personal success, and for that of her *salon*, well and good, but her interest stops there.

Célimène is young, gay, sparkling, attractive, so that we can well understand her fascination for Alceste. But, despite all her charms, she is selfish, superficial, and insincere. It is difficult to believe that so many could be deceived by her, but they, doubtless, in their turn showed just the same characteristics. Sincerity, Molière is careful to point out, was not much in evidence in Court circles. Typical of Célimène's duplicity is her remark to Arsinoé, whom she has been criticizing with some vehemence : "Ah ! quel heureux sort en ce lieu vous amène ? " (Act III, Scene 4). Touches such as this reveal Molière's perspicacity and insight into the minds of his characters. To do Célimène justice, it must, however, be noted that at the conclusion of the play, when confronted by Alceste, she admits with what appears to be genuine sincerity and contrition, " . . . je tombe d'accord de mon crime envers vous." Unfortunately this change of heart is of a purely temporary nature. It should, of course, always be borne in mind that Célimène is a very young woman, and that it would be hardly natural to expect her to settle down with a man of Alceste's temperament. We do not know Alceste's exact age, but it is obvious he is older than Célimène in both years and experience.

The truth is that Célimène's conception of love is not whole-hearted devotion or passion, but the gratification of her own caprices in the admiration and attentions of the men who surround her. She is the exact opposite of the *grande amoureuse* of the Romantic writers. Indeed, love which entailed any sacrifice or renunciation is unthinkable in her case.

Molière's studies of women in *Le Misanthrope* are particularly distinguished. After Célimène we have two excellently drawn feminine portraits: Arsinoé and Éliante. While we have noted certain points in Célimène's favour, it would be difficult to find any redeeming features in the case of her prudish rival, Arsinoé. The very name, borrowed from Corneille's *Nicomède*, is synonymous with all that is crafty, vindictive, and small-minded. Molière himself seems to have had a particular antipathy for such women, and his study inspires the same feeling in the reader. Women of this type had been largely responsible for the adverse criticism of *L'École des Femmes*, and in his *Critique* he denounces " celles qui, étant sur le retour de l'âge . . . prétendent que les grimaces d'une pruderie scrupuleuse leur tiendront lieu de jeunesse et de beauté."

In comparison with Arsinoé, Célimène appears almost likeable and honest, and the prude certainly meets her match in her young rival. Maybe for one fleeting moment the reader does feel some pity for the unhappy Arsinoé when she leaves Célimène after their famous dialogue. In her heart Arsinoé envies Célimène's success and suitors : her prudery is merely a defence mechanism—the only available weapon for this embittered and disillusioned woman. There is no doubt that the scene between Célimène and Arsinoé is one of the most brilliant that Molière ever wrote.

To balance the two extremes, Célimène and Arsinoé, Molière introduces Éliante—perhaps his conception of the sane, sensible, average woman. Natural, honest, and simple, Éliante shows those qualities of tolerance and patience which we noted in Philinte. We feel that a match between Éliante and Philinte is destined to be successful. Certain critics have questioned the depth of her feelings, especially as she seems willing to give her hand either to Alceste or Philinte, but the reader realizes that in the case of Alceste her action is a mere gesture of sympathy and understanding, and that Philinte is the one who will eventually win her.

The remaining important characters, Oronte, Acaste, and Clitandre, are masterly studies of true types observed by Molière. We have already seen, in the general introduction, that Molière wished to satirize courtiers and Court life in *Le Misanthrope*, and these personages afford him an excellent opportunity of so doing. Oronte is the type *par excellence* of the would-be poet in Court circles. It was the fashion for young nobles to write poetry—or what they thought was poetry—and it was likewise the fashion to expect praise. Men of real talent were frequently excluded from aristocratic *salons* if they were not of noble birth, while mediocre versifiers were overwhelmed with praise and flattery, which caused them to believe themselves really gifted. Molière wished to satirize these Court poets, not only because they were ridiculous, but also because they were a potential danger to the talented professional writer.

The two *petits marquis*, Acaste and Clitandre, introduce a light-hearted note into the play. Their fashionable jargon, exaggerated interest in clothes and appearance, their conceit and utter fatuity, are responsible for much merriment and comic relief, without which the play would tend to become over-serious. The foppish type of *marquis* must have been the subject of constant mirth on the stage, for Molière writes in *L'Impromptu de Versailles*: "Le marquis aujourd'hui est le plaisant de la comédie ; et comme, dans toutes les comédies anciennes, on voit toujours un valet bouffon qui fait rire les auditeurs, de même, dans toutes nos pièces de maintenant, il faut toujours un marquis ridicule qui divertisse la compagnie."

The lives of courtiers such as Acaste and Clitandre were governed by one thing only—*la mode*. Fashion dictated what they should wear, how they should speak, where they should show themselves off, almost how they should think ; and so in his two *petits marquis* Molière satirizes a whole section of contemporary society, a whole way of living.

Similarly, in his studies of the other characters whom we have discussed, Molière reviews types which not only throw light on Molière's own contemporaries, but which symbolize men and women of every century. We have not far to look in our own time to find the modern counterparts of Alceste, Philinte, Célimène, Arsinoé, and other characters in the play. Rigal in his searching study of *Le Misanthrope* fittingly writes : "*Le Misanthrope*, ce n'est rien de moins qu'une étude presque complète de la société contemporaine et de l'humanité."

## 5. A Note on French Versification

*By R. P. L. Ledésert*

Lyrical poetry in France in the sixteenth century flourished under the leadership of Ronsard, who introduced new stanzas and hitherto unfamiliar forms of poetic expression. But it is characteristic of the less spontaneous seventeenth century that more emphasis should have been laid on the importance of form, establishing for the first time in the history of French literature definite rules of versification.

The literary critics of the century laid too much emphasis, perhaps, on what we would consider minor details, such as the position of the cæsura, or the famous *enjambement* which was to excite so much rebellion among Romantics almost two centuries later. And in illustration of this we cannot do better than to quote here the leading seventeenth-century French critic, Boileau :

N'offrez rien au lecteur que ce qui peut lui plaire,
Ayez pour la cadence une oreille sévère,
Que toujours dans vos vers, le sens coupant les mots
Suspende l'hémistiche, en marque le repos.
Gardez qu'une voyelle à courir trop hâtée,
Ne soit d'une voyelle en son chemin heurtée.

(*L'Art Poétique*, Chant I, lines 103 *et seq.*)

The rules of French versification, though contained in the lines quoted above, are not quite so simple as they may appear, and it may be that a few words of explanation are not out of place here.

### 1. Scansion.

Each verse is divided into a certain number of *pieds*. The *pied* in French versification corresponds to a single syllable and not to the group of syllables known as *foot* in English poetry:

| Les | uns, | par | ce | qu'ils | sont | mé | chants | et | mal | fai | sants |
|---|---|---|---|---|---|---|---|---|---|---|---|
| 1 | 2 | 3 | 4 | 5 | 6 | 7 | 8 | 9 | 10 | 11 | 12 |

(MOLIÈRE, *Le Misanthrope*, Act I, Scene 1)

2. MUTE E (*e muet*).

(*a*) When a mute *e* appears in a syllable placed at the end of a word in the body of a line, two cases are to be considered:

(i) when the mute *e* is followed by a consonant, it is counted as a *pied*:

| J'o | se | m'i | ma | gi | ner | qu'à | ses | moin | dres | ex | ploits |
|---|---|---|---|---|---|---|---|---|---|---|---|
| 1 | 2 | 3 | 4 | 5 | 6 | 7 | 8 | 9 | 10 | 11 | 12 |

(CORNEILLE, *Le Cid*, Act II, Scene 5)

(ii) when the mute *e* is followed by a word beginning with a vowel or *h* mute, the syllable in which it is contained is not counted as a *pied*:

| Et, | com | me il | voit | en | nous | des | â | mes | peu | com | munes |
|---|---|---|---|---|---|---|---|---|---|---|---|
| 1 | 2 | 3 | 4 | 5 | 6 | 7 | 8 | 9 | 10 | 11 | 12 |

(CORNEILLE, *Horace*, Act II, Scene 3)

(*b*) When a syllable placed at the end of a word at the end of a line contains a mute *e*, it is not counted as a *pied*:

| Nous | se | rons | les | mi | roirs | d'u | ne | ver | tu | bien | rare |
|---|---|---|---|---|---|---|---|---|---|---|---|
| 1 | 2 | 3 | 4 | 5 | 6 | 7 | 8 | 9 | 10 | 11 | 12 |

(CORNEILLE, *Horace*, Act II, Scene 3)

This applies even if the *e* is followed by *s* or *nt*:

| Et, | com | me il | voit | en | nous | des | â | mes | peu | com | munes |
|---|---|---|---|---|---|---|---|---|---|---|---|
| 1 | 2 | 3 | 4 | 5 | 6 | 7 | 8 | 9 | 10 | 11 | 12 |

3. METRE (*mètre*).

(*a*) The line of 12 syllables was the type of verse most commonly used in the seventeenth century. It is known as the *alexandrin*, a name which is believed to originate from *Le Roman d'Alexandre* (twelfth century), which employed a primitive form of this verse.

But other types of metre were nevertheless used in the seventeenth century.

(*b*) The 10-syllable line:

| Puis | qu'au | jour | d'hui | mon | pè | re est | l'of | fen | sé |
|---|---|---|---|---|---|---|---|---|---|
| 1 | 2 | 3 | 4 | 5 | 6 | 7 | 8 | 9 | 10 |

(CORNEILLE, *Le Cid*, Act I, Scene 6)

(*c*) The 8-syllable line:

| Per | cé | jus | ques | au | fond | du | cœur |
|---|---|---|---|---|---|---|---|
| 1 | 2 | 3 | 4 | 5 | 6 | 7 | 8 |

(CORNEILLE, *Le Cid*, Act I, Scene 6)

(*d*) The 7-syllable line:

| Dont | le | ré | cit | est | men | teur |
|---|---|---|---|---|---|---|
| 1 | 2 | 3 | 4 | 5 | 6 | 7 |

(LA FONTAINE)

(*e*) The 6-syllable line, which is sometimes a half-alexandrine:

| Cè | de au | coup | qui | me | tue |
|---|---|---|---|---|---|
| 1 | 2 | 3 | 4 | 5 | 6 |

(CORNEILLE, *Le Cid*, Act I, Scene 6)

Other types of metre were rarely used in the seventeenth century.

4. RHYME (*rime*).

The rhyme consists of the recurrence in the last syllable of a line of the sound found at the end of the preceding line. The essential of French rhyme is to achieve similarity of sound and appearance, with the result that words are held to rhyme in French which to an English ear would appear not to do so. Moreover, the rhyme can consist of identical last syllables of polysyllabic words:

Une vaine frayeur tantôt m'a pu trou*bler*,
Et je suis insensible alors qu'il faut trem*bler*.

There are two main types of rhyme:

(*a*) The *feminine* rhyme where the last syllable is mute:

Pour grands que soient les rois, ils sont ce que nous *sommes*,
Ils peuvent se tromper comme les autres *hommes*.

(CORNEILLE, *Le Cid*, Act I, Scene 3)

(*b*) The *masculine* rhyme in which the last syllable is sounded:

Mourir pour le pays est un si digne *sort*,
Qu'on briguerait en foule une si belle *mort*.

(CORNEILLE, *Horace*, Act II, Scene 3)

But each of these types of rhyme is subdivided into two further groups:

If the syllable of which the rhyme consists begins with the same consonant in the two lines, that is to say, if the two last syllables are identical, the rhyme is called *riche*.

Thus, a *rime féminine riche* is:

Madame, je sais trop à quel excès de *rage*
La vengeance d'Hélène emporta mon cou*rage*.

(RACINE, *Andromaque*, Act IV, Scene 5)

While a *rime masculine riche* is:

Achevez votre hymen, i'y consens ; mais du *moins*,
Ne forcez pas mes yeux d'en être les té*moins*,

(RACINE, *Andromaque*, Act IV, Scene 5)

On the other hand, if the consonants are different, the thyme is called *suffisante*:

> Vous ne répondez point ! Perfide, je le *voi*,
> Tu comptes les moments que tu perds avec *moi* !
>
> (RACINE, *Andromaque*, Act IV, Scene 5)

This is a ***rime masculine suffisante.***

5. CÆSURA (*la césure*).

The ideal alexandrine line is divided into two equal parts of six *pieds* each by the cæsura. Each of these half-alexandrines is called an *hémistiche*, and the break (or cæsura) must not occur in the middle of a word:

| J'ai vu trancher les jours | de ma famille entière |
|---|---|
| 1st hemistich | 2nd hemistich |

| Et mon époux sanglant | traîné sur la poussière |
|---|---|
| 1st hemistich | 2nd hemistich |

(RACINE, *Andromaque*, Act III, Scene 6)

Thus the voice rests at the end of the sixth syllable, and then at the end of the line. This accounts for the apparent monotony of French classical verse to an inexperienced ear.

6. ENJAMBEMENT.

The term *enjambement* is applied to denote a phrase which begins at the end of one line and is continued at the beginning of the next. Though this was forbidden by the critics in the seventeenth century, La Fontaine used it quite frequently:

> Sire, répond l'agneau, *que votre Majesté*
> *Ne se mette pas en colère.*
>
> (LA FONTAINE, *Le Loup et l'Agneau*)

7. HIATUS.

The hiatus was also forbidden by the seventeenth-century critics. It occurs when an accented vowel placed at the end of a word is followed by another accented vowel beginning the following word; or, as Boileau expressed it:

> Gardez qu'une voyelle à courir trop hâtée,
> Ne soit d'une voyelle en son chemin heurtée.

Frequent examples of hiatus are to be found in the poetry of the Middle Ages or of the Renaissance:

> Semblablement, *où est* la royne
> Qui commanda que Buridan
> Fust gec*té en* ung sac en Saine !

(VILLON, *Ballade des Dames du Temps Jadis*)

8. THE ALTERNATION OF MASCULINE AND FEMININE RHYMES IN ALEXANDRINE VERSE.

The accepted rule in the seventeenth century was that couplets ending with masculine rhymes should alternate with couplets ending with feminine rhymes:

Oui, je viens dans son temple adorer l'Éternel :<br>Je viens, selon l'usage antique et solennel, } *masc.*<br>Célébrer avec vous la fameuse journée<br>Où sur le mont Sina la loi nous fut donnée. } *fem.*<br>Que les temps sont changés ! Sitôt que de ce jour<br>La trompette sacrée annonçait le retour, } *masc.*<br>Du temple, orné partout de festons magnifiques,<br>Le peuple saint en foule inondait les portiques ; } *fem.*

(RACINE, *Athalie*, Act I, Scene 1)

There are many other intricacies of French versification. This is not the place to discuss them. The purpose of this note is to enable the reader to understand and appreciate the main principles of French versification. For deeper study reference should be made to Martinon's *Les Strophes*.

## Suggestions for Further Reading and Reference

### I. THE COMPLETE WORKS OF MOLIÈRE

Editions of Molière's works are numerous. The edition published in the " Collection des Grands Écrivains de la France " (Hachette, 1873–93), edited by Eugène Despois and Paul Mesnard, may be regarded as the standard edition of the complete works of Molière. This text is based on it.

There are several other adequate and cheaper French editions, such as that in the " Collection des classiques Garnier."

### II. MOLIÈRE'S LIFE AND WORKS

(*complete books and critical studies*)

ASHTON, H. : *Molière* (Routledge, 1930).

BENJAMIN, R. : *Molière* (Plon, 1936).

BRISSON, P. : *Molière, sa Vie dans ses Œuvres* (Gallimard, 1942).

BRUNETIÈRE, F. : *Études critiques*, vol. iv (Hachette, 1890). See also *Les Époques du Théâtre français* (1901), and vol. viii of the *Études*.

BRUYELLE, R. : *Les Personnages de la Comédie de Molière* (Debresse, 1946).

DONNAY, M. : *Molière* (Fayard, 1911).

FAGUET, E. : *Dix-septième Siècle*, in " Études littéraires " (Lecène, Oudin, 1885 *et seq.*). See also his excellent critical study *En lisant Molière* (Hachette, 1914).

FERNANDEZ, R. : *La Vie de Molière* (Éditions de la Nouvelle Revue Française, 1929).

LANCASTER, H. : *A History of French Dramatic Literature in the Seventeenth Century, Part III : The Period of Molière* 1652–1672, 2 vols. (Baltimore, Johns Hopkins, 1936).

LARROUMET, C. : *La Comédie de Molière* (Hachette, 1886).

MICHAUT, G. : *La Jeunesse de Molière* (Hachette, 1922).

MICHAUT, G. : *Les Débuts de Molière à Paris* (Hachette, 1923).

MICHAUT, G. : *Les grandes Luttes de Molière* (Hachette, 1925).

MICHAUT, G. : *Le Triomphe de Molière* (Hachette, 1927).

RIGAL, E. : *Molière* (Hachette, 1908), 2 vols.

STAPFER, P.: *Molière et Shakespeare* (Hachette, 1899).

TURNELL, M.: *The Classical Moment* (Hamish Hamilton, 1947).

*Molière, Encyclopédie par l'image* (Hachette, 1926).

## III. MOLIÈRE'S AGE AND BACKGROUND

ASHTON, H.: *Preface to Molière* (Longmans, 1927).

BOULANGER, J.: *Le Grand Siècle* (Hachette).

BRAUNSCHVIG, M.: *Notre Littérature étudiée dans les Textes*, tome Ier (Armand Colin).

LAVISSE, E.: *Histoire de France depuis les Origines jusqu'à la Révolution* (Hachette, 1901–7).

LEDÉSERT, R. P. L. and D. M.: *Histoire de la Littérature française*, tome Ier (Arnold, 1946).

MALET ET ISAAC: *XVIIe et XVIIIe Siècles* (Hachette).

MORNET, D.: *Histoire de la Littérature française classique*, 1660–1700 (Armand Colin, 1947).

STRACHEY, G. LYTTON: *Landmarks in French Literature* ("Home University Library," Oxford University Press).

# LE MISANTHROPE

## ACTEURS

ALCESTE, amant de Célimène.

PHILINTE, ami d'Alceste.

ORONTE, amant de Célimène.

CÉLIMÈNE, amante d'Alceste.

ÉLIANTE, cousine de Célimène.

ARSINOÉ, amie de Célimène.

ACASTE,<br>CLITANDRE, } marquis.

BASQUE, valet de Célimène.

UN GARDE de la maréchaussée de France.

DUBOIS, valet d'Alceste.

*La scène est à Paris.*

# ACTE I

## SCÈNE PREMIÈRE

*Philinte, Alceste*

PHILINTE. Qu'est-ce donc ? Qu'avez-vous ?
ALCESTE. Laissez-moi,
je vous prie.
PHILINTE. Mais encor dites-moi quelle bizarrerie. . . .
ALCESTE. Laissez-moi là, vous dis-je, et courez vous cacher. 5
PHILINTE. Mais on entend les gens, au moins, sans se fâcher.
ALCESTE. Moi, je veux me fâcher, et ne veux point entendre. 10
PHILINTE. Dans vos brusques chagrins je ne puis vous comprendre,
Et quoique amis enfin, je suis tout des premiers. . . .
ALCESTE. Moi, votre ami ? Rayez cela de vos papiers.
J'ai fait jusques ici profession de l'être ; 15
Mais après ce qu'en vous je viens de voir paraître,
Je vous déclare net que je ne le suis plus,
Et ne veux nulle place en des cœurs corrompus.
PHILINTE. Je suis donc bien coupable, Alceste, à votre compte ? 20
ALCESTE. Allez, vous devriez mourir de pure honte :
Une telle action ne saurait s'excuser,
Et tout homme d'honneur s'en doit scandaliser.
Je vous vois accabler un homme de caresses,
Et témoigner pour lui les dernières tendresses ; 25
De protestations, d'offres et de serments,
Vous chargez la fureur de vos embrassements ;

ALCESTE

*Laissez-moi, je vous prie.*

Et quand je vous demande après quel est cet homme,
A peine pouvez-vous dire comme il se nomme ;
Votre chaleur pour lui tombe en vous séparant,
Et vous me le traitez, à moi, d'indifférent.
Morbleu ! c'est une chose indigne, lâche, infâme, 5
De s'abaisser ainsi jusqu'à trahir son âme ;
Et si, par un malheur, j'en avais fait autant,
Je m'irais, de regret, pendre tout à l'instant.

PHILINTE. Je ne vois pas, pour moi, que le cas soit pendable, 10
Et je vous supplierai d'avoir pour agréable
Que je me fasse un peu grâce sur votre arrêt,
Et ne me pende pas pour cela, s'il vous plaît.

ALCESTE. Que la plaisanterie est de mauvaise grâce !

PHILINTE. Mais, sérieusement, que voulez-vous qu'on fasse ? 15

ALCESTE. Je veux qu'on soit sincère, et qu'en homme d'honneur,
On ne lâche aucun mot qui ne parte du cœur.

PHILINTE. Lorsqu'un homme vous vient embrasser avec joie, 20
Il faut bien le payer de la même monnoie,
Répondre, comme on peut, à ses empressements,
Et rendre offre pour offre, et serments pour serments.

ALCESTE. Non, je ne puis souffrir cette lâche méthode 25
Qu'affectent la plupart de vos gens à la mode ;
Et je ne hais rien tant que les contorsions
De tous ces grands faiseurs de protestations,
Ces affables donneurs d'embrassades frivoles,
Ces obligeants diseurs d'inutiles paroles, 30
Qui de civilités avec tous font combat,
Et traitent du même air l'honnête homme et le fat.
Quel avantage a-t-on qu'un homme vous caresse,
Vous jure amitié, foi, zèle, estime, tendresse,
Et vous fasse de vous un éloge éclatant, 35

Lorsqu'au premier faquin il court en faire autant ?
Non, non, il n'est point d'âme un peu bien située
Qui veuille d'une estime ainsi prostituée ;
Et la plus glorieuse a des régals peu chers,
Dès qu'on voit qu'on nous mêle avec tout l'univers : 5
Sur quelque préférence une estime se fonde,
Et c'est n'estimer rien qu'estimer tout le monde.
Puisque vous y donnez, dans ces vices du temps,
Morbleu ! vous n'êtes pas pour être de mes gens ;
Je refuse d'un cœur la vaste complaisance 10
Qui ne fait de mérite aucune différence ;
Je veux qu'on me distingue et pour le trancher net,
L'ami du genre humain n'est point du tout mon fait.

PHILINTE. Mais, quand on est du monde, il faut bien que l'on rende 15
Quelques dehors civils que l'usage demande.

ALCESTE. Non, vous dis-je, on devrait châtier sans pitié
Ce commerce honteux de semblants d'amitié.
Je veux que l'on soit homme, et qu'en toute rencontre
Le fond de notre cœur dans nos discours se montre, 20
Que ce soit lui qui parle, et que nos sentiments
Ne se masquent jamais sous de vains compliments.

PHILINTE. Il est bien des endroits où la pleine franchise
Deviendrait ridicule et serait peu permise ;
Et parfois, n'en déplaise à votre austère honneur, 25
Il est bon de cacher ce qu'on a dans le cœur.
Serait-il à propos et de la bienséance
De dire à mille gens tout ce que d'eux on pense ?
Et quand on a quelqu'un qu'on hait ou qui déplaît,
Lui doit-on déclarer la chose comme elle est ? 30

ALCESTE. Oui.

PHILINTE. Quoi ! vous iriez dire à la vieille Émilie
Qu'à son âge il sied mal de faire la jolie,
Et que le blanc qu'elle a scandalise chacun ?

ALCESTE. Sans doute. 35

PHILINTE. A Dorilas, qu'il est trop importun,
Et qu'il n'est à la cour oreille qu'il ne lasse
A conter sa bravoure et l'éclat de sa race?
ALCESTE. Fort bien.
PHILINTE. Vous vous moquez. 5
ALCESTE. Je ne me moque point.
Et je vais n'épargner personne sur ce point.
Mes yeux sont trop blessés, et la cour et la ville
Ne m'offrent rien qu'objets à m'échauffer la bile; 10
J'entre en une humeur noire, en un chagrin profond,
Quand je vois vivre entre eux les hommes comme ils font;
Je ne trouve partout que lâche flatterie,
Qu'injustice, intérêt, trahison, fourberie: 15
Je n'y puis plus tenir, j'enrage, et mon dessein
Est de rompre en visière à tout le genre humain.
PHILINTE. Ce chagrin philosophe est un peu trop sauvage,
Je ris des noirs accès où je vous envisage,
Et crois voir en nous deux, sous mêmes soins nourris, 20
Ces deux frères que peint *l'École des maris*,
Dont. . .
ALCESTE. Mon Dieu! laissons là vos comparaisons fades.
PHILINTE. Non: tout de bon, quittez toutes ces incartades.
Le monde par vos soins ne se changera pas: 25
Et puisque la franchise a pour vous tant d'appas,
Je vous dirai tout franc que cette maladie,
Partout où vous allez, donne la comédie,
Et qu'un si grand courroux contre les mœurs du temps
Vous tourne en ridicule auprès de bien des gens. 30
ALCESTE. Tant mieux, morbleu! tant mieux, c'est ce que je demande;
Ce m'est un fort bon signe, et ma joie en est grande:
Tous les hommes me sont à tel point odieux,
Que je serais fâché d'être sage à leurs yeux. 35

PHILINTE. Vous voulez un grand mal à la nature humaine.
ALCESTE. Oui, j'ai conçu pour elle une effroyable haine.
PHILINTE. Tous les pauvres mortels, sans nulle exception,
Seront enveloppés dans cette aversion ?
Encore en est-il bien, dans le siècle où nous sommes.... 5
ALCESTE. Non : elle est générale, et je hais tous les hommes :
Les uns, parce qu'ils sont méchants et malfaisants,
Et les autres, pour être aux méchants complaisants,
Et n'avoir pas pour eux ces haines vigoureuses 10
Que doit donner le vice aux âmes vertueuses.
De cette complaisance on voit l'injuste excès
Pour le franc scélérat avec qui j'ai procès :
Au travers de son masque on voit à plein le traître ;
Partout il est connu pour tout ce qu'il peut être ; 15
Et ses roulements d'yeux, et son ton radouci,
N'imposent qu'à des gens qui ne sont point d'ici.
On sait que ce pied plat, digne qu'on le confonde,
Par de sales emplois s'est poussé dans le monde,
Et que par eux son sort, de splendeur revêtu, 20
Fait gronder le mérite et rougir la vertu.
Quelques titres honteux qu'en tous lieux on lui donne,
Son misérable honneur ne voit pour lui personne ;
Nommez-le fourbe, infâme, et scélérat maudit,
Tout le monde en convient, et nul n'y contredit, 25
Cependant sa grimace est partout bienvenue ;
On l'accueille, on lui rit, partout il s'insinue ;
Et s'il est, par la brigue, un rang à disputer,
Sur le plus honnête homme on le voit l'emporter.
Têtebleu ! ce me sont de mortelles blessures, 30
De voir qu'avec le vice on garde des mesures ;
Et parfois il me prend des mouvements soudains
De fuir dans un désert l'approche des humains.
PHILINTE. Mon Dieu ! des mœurs du temps mettons-nous moins en peine, 35

Et faisons un peu grâce à la nature humaine ;
Ne l'examinons point dans la grande rigueur,
Et voyons ses défauts avec quelque douceur.
Il faut, parmi le monde, une vertu traitable ;
A force de sagesse, on peut être blâmable ; 5
La parfaite raison fuit toute extrémité,
Et veut que l'on soit sage avec sobriété.
Cette grande roideur des vertus des vieux âges
Heurte trop notre siècle et les communs usages ;
Elle veut aux mortels trop de perfection : 10
Il faut fléchir au temps sans obstination;
Et c'est une folie à nulle autre seconde,
De vouloir se mêler de corriger le monde.
J'observe, comme vous, cent choses tous les jours,
Qui pourraient mieux aller, prenant un autre cours : 15
Mais quoi qu'à chaque pas je puisse voir paraître,
En courroux, comme vous, on ne me voit point être ;
Je prends tout doucement les hommes comme ils sont,
J'accoutume mon âme à souffrir ce qu'ils font ;
Et je crois qu'à la cour, de même qu'à la ville, 20
Mon flegme est philosophe autant que votre bile.

ALCESTE. Mais ce flegme, monsieur, qui raisonne si bien,
Ce flegme pourra-t-il ne s'échauffer de rien ?
Et s'il faut, par hasard, qu'un ami vous trahisse,
Que, pour avoir vos biens, on dresse un artifice, 25
Ou qu'on tâche à semer de méchants bruits de vous,
Verrez-vous tout cela sans vous mettre en courroux ?

PHILINTE. Oui, je vois ces défauts dont votre âme murmure
Comme vices unis à l'humaine nature ; 30
Et mon esprit enfin n'est pas plus offensé
De voir un homme fourbe, injuste, intéressé,
Que de voir des vautours affamés de carnage,
Des singes malfaisants, et des loups pleins de rage.

ALCESTE. Je me verrai trahir, mettre en pièces, voler. 35

Sans que je sois. . . . Morbleu ! je ne veux point parler,
Tant ce raisonnement est plein d'impertinence.

PHILINTE. Ma foi ! vous ferez bien de garder le silence.
Contre votre partie éclatez un peu moins, 5
Et donnez au procès une part de vos soins.

ALCESTE. Je n'en donnerai point, c'est une chose dite.

PHILINTE. Mais qui voulez-vous donc qui pour vous sollicite ?

ALCESTE. Qui je veux ? La raison, mon bon droit, l'équité. 10

PHILINTE. Aucun juge par vous ne sera visité ?

ALCESTE. Non. Est-ce que ma cause est injuste ou douteuse ?

PHILINTE. J'en demeure d'accord ; mais la brigue est fâcheuse, 15
Et. . . .

ALCESTE. Non : j'ai résolu de n'en pas faire un pas.
J'ai tort, ou j'ai raison.

PHILINTE. Ne vous y fiez pas. 20

ALCESTE. Je ne remuerai point.

PHILINTE. Votre partie est forte,
Et peut, par sa cabale, entraîner. . . .

ALCESTE. Il n'importe.

PHILINTE. Vous vous tromperez. 25

ALCESTE. Soit. J'en veux voir le succès.

PHILINTE. Mais . . .

ALCESTE. J'aurai le plaisir de perdre mon procès. 30

PHILINTE. Mais enfin . . .

ALCESTE. Je verrai, dans cette plaiderie,
Si les hommes auront assez d'effronterie,
Seront assez méchants, scélérats et pervers,
Pour me faire injustice aux yeux de l'univers. 35

PHILINTE. Quel homme !

ALCESTE. Je voudrais, m'en coûtât-il grand'chose,
Pour la beauté du fait avoir perdu ma cause.

PHILINTE. On se rirait de vous, Alceste, tout de bon, 5
Si l'on vous entendait parler de la façon.

ALCESTE. Tant pis pour qui rirait.

PHILINTE. Mais cette rectitude
Que vous voulez en tout avec exactitude,
Cette pleine droiture, où vous vous renfermez, 10
La trouvez-vous ici dans ce que vous aimez?
Je m'étonne, pour moi, qu'étant, comme il le semble,
Vous et le genre humain si fort brouillés ensemble,
Malgré tout ce qui peut vous le rendre odieux,
Vous ayez pris chez lui ce qui charme vos yeux; 15
Et ce qui me surprend encore davantage,
C'est cet étrange choix où votre cœur s'engage.
La sincère Éliante a du penchant pour vous,
La prude Arsinoé vous voit d'un œil fort doux;
Cependant à leurs vœux votre âme se refuse, 20
Tandis qu'en ses liens Célimène l'amuse,
De qui l'humeur coquette et l'esprit médisant
Semblent si fort donner dans les mœurs d'à présent.
D'où vient que, leur portant une haine mortelle,
Vous pouvez bien souffrir ce qu'en tient cette belle? 25
Ne sont-ce plus défauts dans un objet si doux?
Ne les voyez-vous pas? ou les excusez-vous?

ALCESTE. Non. L'amour que je sens pour cette jeune veuve
Ne ferme point mes yeux aux défauts qu'on lui treuve, 30
Et je suis, quelque ardeur qu'elle m'ait pu donner,
Le premier à les voir, comme à les condamner.
Mais, avec tout cela, quoi que je puisse faire,
Je confesse mon faible, elle a l'art de me plaire:
J'ai beau voir ses défauts, et j'ai beau l'en blâmer, 35

En dépit qu'on en ait, elle se fait aimer;
Sa grâce est la plus forte ; et sans doute ma flamme
De ces vices du temps pourra purger son âme.

PHILINTE. Si vous faites cela, vous ne ferez pas peu.
Vous croyez être donc aimé d'elle ? 5

ALCESTE. Oui, parbleu !
Je ne l'aimerais pas, si je ne croyais l'être.

PHILINTE. Mais, si son amitié pour vous se fait paraître,
D'où vient que vos rivaux vous causent de l'ennui ?

ALCESTE. C'est qu'un cœur bien atteint veut qu'on soit tout à lui, 10
Et je ne viens ici qu'à dessein de lui dire
Tout ce que là-dessus ma passion m'inspire.

PHILINTE. Pour moi, si je n'avais qu'à former des désirs,
La cousine Éliante aurait tous mes soupirs ; 15
Son cœur, qui vous estime, est solide et sincère,
Et ce choix plus conforme était mieux votre affaire.

ALCESTE. Il est vrai : ma raison me le dit chaque jour ;
Mais la raison n'est pas ce qui règle l'amour.

PHILINTE. Je crains fort pour vos feux, et l'espoir où vous êtes 20
Pourrait. . . .

## SCÈNE II

*Oronte, Alceste, Philinte*

ORONTE. J'ai su là-bas que, pour quelques emplettes,
Éliante est sortie, et Célimène aussi ; 25
Mais comme l'on m'a dit que vous étiez ici,
J'ai monté pour vous dire, et d'un cœur véritable,
Que j'ai conçu pour vous une estime incroyable,
Et que, depuis longtemps, cette estime m'a mis
Dans un ardent désir d'être de vos amis. 30

Oui, mon cœur au mérite aime à rendre justice,
Et je brûle qu'un nœud d'amitié nous unisse :
Je crois qu'un ami chaud, et de ma qualité,
N'est pas assurément pour être rejeté.
C'est à vous, s'il vous plaît, que ce discours s'adresse. 5
[*En cet endroit Alceste paraît tout rêveur, et semble ne pas entendre qu'Oronte lui parle.*]

ALCESTE. A moi, monsieur ?
ORONTE. A vous. Trouvez-vous qu'il vous blesse ? 10
ALCESTE. Non pas ; mais la surprise est fort grande pour moi,
Et je n'attendais pas l'honneur que je reçoi.
ORONTE. L'estime où je vous tiens ne doit point vous surprendre, 15
Et de tout l'univers vous la pouvez prétendre.
ALCESTE. Monsieur. . . .
ORONTE. L'État n'a rien qui ne soit au-dessous
Du mérite éclatant que l'on découvre en vous. 20
ALCESTE. Monsieur. . . .
ORONTE. Oui, de ma part, je vous tiens préférable
A tout ce que j'y vois de plus considérable.
ALCESTE. Monsieur. . . . 25
ORONTE. Sois-je du ciel écrasé, si je mens !
Et pour vous confirmer ici mes sentiments,
Souffrez qu'à cœur ouvert, monsieur, je vous embrasse,
Et qu'en votre amitié je vous demande place.
Touchez là, s'il vous plaît. Vous me la promettez, 30
Votre amitié ?
ALCESTE. Monsieur. . . .
ORONTE. Quoi ? vous y résistez ?
ALCESTE. Monsieur, c'est trop d'honneur que vous me voulez faire : 35

Mais l'amitié demande un peu plus de mystère,
Et c'est assurément en profaner le nom
Que de vouloir le mettre à toute occasion.
Avec lumière et choix cette union veut naître ;
Avant que nous lier, il faut nous mieux connaître ; 5
Et nous pourrions avoir telles complexions,
Que tous deux du marché nous nous repentirions.

ORONTE. Parbleu ! c'est là-dessus parler en homme sage,
Et je vous en estime encore davantage :
Souffrons donc que le temps forme des nœuds si doux ; 10
Mais, cependant, je m'offre entièrement à vous :
S'il faut faire à la cour pour vous quelque ouverture,
On sait qu'auprès du Roi je fais quelque figure ;
Il m'écoute ; et dans tout, il en use, ma foi !
Le plus honnêtement du monde avecque moi. 15
Enfin je suis à vous de toutes les manières ;
Et comme votre esprit a de grandes lumières,
Je viens, pour commencer entre nous ce beau nœud,
Vous montrer un sonnet que j'ai fait depuis peu,
Et savoir s'il est bon qu'au public je l'expose. 20

ALCESTE. Monsieur, je suis mal propre à décider la chose :
Veuillez m'en dispenser.

ORONTE. Pourquoi ?

ALCESTE. J'ai le défaut
D'être un peu plus sincère en cela qu'il ne faut. 25

ORONTE. C'est ce que je demande, et j'aurais lieu de plainte,
Si, m'exposant à vous pour me parler sans feinte,
Vous alliez me trahir, et me déguiser rien.

ALCESTE. Puisqu'il vous plaît ainsi, monsieur, je le veux bien. 30

ORONTE. *Sonnet*. . . . C'est un sonnet. *L'espoir*. . . . C'est une dame
Qui de quelque espérance avait flatté ma flamme.
*L'espoir*. . . . Ce ne sont point de ces grands vers pompeux, 35

Mais de petits vers doux, tendres et langoureux.
[*A toutes ces interruptions il regarde Alceste.*]

ALCESTE. Nous verrons bien.

ORONTE. *L'espoir. . .* Je ne sais si le style 5
Pourra vous en paraître assez net et facile,
Et si du choix des mots vous vous contenterez.

ALCESTE. Nous allons voir, monsieur.

ORONTE. Au reste, vous saurez
Que je n'ai demeuré qu'un quart d'heure à le faire. 10

ALCESTE. Voyons, monsieur ; le temps ne fait rien à l'affaire.

ORONTE.
*L'espoir, il est vrai, nous soulage,*
*Et nous berce un temps notre ennui ;*
*Mais, Philis, le triste avantage,* 15
*Lorsque rien ne marche après lui !*

PHILINTE. Je suis déjà charmé de ce petit morceau.

ALCESTE. Quoi ? vous avez le front de trouver cela beau ?

ORONTE.
*Vous eûtes de la complaisance ;* 20
*Mais vous en deviez moins avoir,*
*Et ne vous pas mettre en dépense*
*Pour ne me donner que l'espoir.*

PHILINTE. Ah ! qu'en termes galants ces choses-là sont mises ! 25

ALCESTE, *bas*. Morbleu ! vil complaisant, vous louez des sottises ?

ORONTE.
*S'il faut qu'une attente éternelle*
*Pousse à bout l'ardeur de mon zèle,*
*Le trépas sera mon recours.* 30

*Vos soins ne m'en peuvent distraire :*
*Belle Philis, on désespère,*
*Alors qu'on espère toujours.*

PHILINTE. La chute en est jolie, amoureuse, admirable.

ALCESTE, *bas*. La peste de ta chute! Empoisonneur au diable,
En eusses-tu fait une à te casser le nez!

PHILINTE. Je n'ai jamais ouï de vers si bien tournés.

ALCESTE. Morbleu! . . . 5

ORONTE. Vous me flattez, et vous croyez peut-être. . . .

PHILINTE. Non, je ne flatte point.

ALCESTE, *bas*. Et que fais-tu donc, traître? 10

ORONTE. Mais, pour vous, vous savez quel est notre traité:
Parlez-moi, je vous prie, avec sincérité.

ALCESTE. Monsieur, cette matière est toujours délicate,
Et sur le bel esprit nous aimons qu'on nous flatte. 15
Mais un jour, à quelqu'un, dont je tairai le nom,
Je disais, en voyant des vers de sa façon,
Qu'il faut qu'un galant homme ait toujours grand empire
Sur les démangeaisons qui nous prennent d'écrire;
Qu'il doit tenir la bride aux grands empressements 20
Qu'on a de faire éclat de tels amusements;
Et que, par la chaleur de montrer ses ouvrages,
On s'expose à jouer de mauvais personnages.

ORONTE. Est-ce que vous voulez me déclarer par là
Que j'ai tort de vouloir. . . ? 25

ALCESTE. Je ne dis pas cela;
Mais, je lui disais, moi, qu'un froid écrit assomme,
Qu'il ne faut que ce faible à décrier un homme,
Et qu'eût-on, d'autre part, cent belles qualités,
On regarde les gens par leurs méchants côtés. 30

ORONTE. Est-ce qu'à mon sonnet vous trouvez à redire?

ALCESTE. Je ne dis pas cela; mais, pour ne point écrire,
Je lui mettais aux yeux comme, dans notre temps,
Cette soif a gâté de fort honnêtes gens.

ORONTE. Est-ce que j'écris mal? et leur ressemblerais-je? 35

ALCESTE. Je ne dis pas cela ; mais enfin, lui disais je,
Quel besoin si pressant avez-vous de rimer ?
Et qui diantre vous pousse à vous faire imprimer ?
Si l'on peut pardonner l'essor d'un mauvais livre,
Ce n'est qu'aux malheureux qui composent pour vivre. 5
Croyez-moi, résistez à vos tentations,
Dérobez au public ces occupations :
Et n'allez point quitter, de quoi que l'on vous somme,
Le nom que dans la cour vous avez d'honnête homme,
Pour prendre, de la main d'un avide imprimeur, 10
Celui de ridicule et misérable auteur.
C'est ce que je tâchai de lui faire comprendre.

ORONTE. Voilà qui va fort bien, et je crois vous entendre.
Mais ne puis-je savoir ce que dans mon sonnet. . . ?

ALCESTE. Franchement, il est bon à mettre au cabinet. 15
Vous vous êtes réglé sur de méchants modèles,
Et vos expressions ne sont point naturelles.
Qu'est-ce que *Nous berce un temps notre ennui ?*
Et que *Rien ne marche après lui ?*
Que *Ne vous pas mettre en dépense* 20
*Pour ne me donner que l'espoir ?*
Et que *Philis, on désespère,*
*Alors qu'on espère toujours ?*
Ce style figuré, dont on fait vanité,
Sort du bon caractère et de la vérité ; 25
Ce n'est que jeu de mots, qu'affectation pure,
Et ce n'est point ainsi que parle la nature.
Le méchant goût du siècle en cela me fait peur.
Nos pères, tout grossiers, l'avaient beaucoup meilleur,
Et je prise bien moins tout ce que l'on admire, 30
Qu'une vieille chanson que je m'en vais vous dire :
*Si le Roi m'avait donné*
*Paris, sa grand' ville,*
*Et qu'il me fallût quitter*
*L'amour de ma mie,* 35

*Je dirais au roi Henri :*
*« Reprenez votre Paris :*
*J'aime mieux ma mie, au gué !*
*J'aime mieux ma mie. »*

La rime n'est pas riche, et le style en est vieux : 5
Mais ne voyez-vous pas que cela vaut bien mieux
Que ces colifichets, dont le bon sens murmure,
Et que la passion parle là toute pure ?

*Si le Roi m'avait donné*
*Paris, sa grand' ville,* 10
*Et qu'il me fallût quitter*
*L'amour de ma mie,*
*Je dirais au roi Henri :*
*« Reprenez votre Paris ;*
*J'aime mieux ma mie, au gué !* 15
*J'aime mieux ma mie. »*

Voilà ce que peut dire un cœur vraiment épris.

*A Philinte.*

Oui, monsieur le rieur, malgré vos beaux esprits,
J'estime plus cela que la pompe fleurie 20
De tous ces faux brillants, où chacun se récrie.

ORONTE. Et moi, je vous soutiens que mes vers sont fort bons.

ALCESTE. Pour les trouver ainsi vous avez vos raisons ;
Mais vous trouverez bon que j'en puisse avoir d'autres, 25
Qui se dispenseront de se soumettre aux vôtres.

ORONTE. Il me suffit de voir que d'autres en font cas.

ALCESTE. C'est qu'ils ont l'art de feindre ; et moi, je ne l'ai pas. 30

ORONTE. Croyez-vous donc avoir tant d'esprit en partage ?

ALCESTE. Si je louais vos vers, j'en aurais davantage.

ORONTE. Je me passerai bien que vous les approuviez.

ALCESTE. Il faut bien, s'il vous plaît, que vous vous en passiez. 35

ORONTE. Je voudrais bien, pour voir, que, de votre manière,
Vous en composassiez sur la même matière.

ALCESTE. J'en pourrais, par malheur, faire d'aussi méchants ; 5
Mais je me garderais de les montrer aux gens.

ORONTE. Vous me parlez bien ferme, et cette suffisance. . . .

ALCESTE. Autre part que chez moi cherchez qui vous encense. 10

ORONTE. Mais, mon petit monsieur, prenez-le un peu moins haut.

ALCESTE. Ma foi ! mon grand monsieur, je le prends comme il faut.

PHILINTE, *se mettant entre-deux*. Eh ! messieurs, c'en est trop ; laissez cela, de grâce. 15

ORONTE. Ah ! j'ai tort, je l'avoue, et je quitte la place.
Je suis votre valet, monsieur, de tout mon cœur.

ALCESTE. Et moi, je suis, monsieur, votre humble serviteur. 20

## SCÈNE III

*Philinte, Alceste*

PHILINTE. Hé bien ! vous le voyez : pour être trop sincère,
Vous voilà sur les bras une fâcheuse affaire ;
Et j'ai bien vu qu'Oronte, afin d'être flatté. . . .

ALCESTE. Ne me parlez pas.

PHILINTE. Mais. . . . 25

ALCESTE. Plus de société.

PHILINTE. C'est trop. . . .

ALCESTE. Laissez-moi là.

PHILINTE. Si je. . .

ALCESTE. Point de langage.
PHILINTE. Mais quoi. . . .
ALCESTE. Je n'entends rien.
PHILINTE. Mais. . . .
ALCESTE. Encore ? 5
PHILINTE. On outrage. . . .
ALCESTE. Ah, parbleu ! c'en est trop ; ne suivez point mes pas.
PHILINTE. Vous vous moquez de moi, je ne vous quitte pas. 10

# ACTE II

## SCÈNE PREMIÈRE

*Alceste, Célimène*

ALCESTE. Madame, voulez-vous que je vous parle net ?
De vos façons d'agir je suis mal satisfait ;
Contre elles dans mon cœur trop de bile s'assemble,
Et je sens qu'il faudra que nous rompions ensemble.
Oui, je vous tromperais de parler autrement ; 5
Tôt ou tard nous romprons indubitablement ;
Et je vous promettrais mille fois le contraire,
Que je ne serais pas en pouvoir de le faire.

CÉLIMÈNE. C'est pour me quereller donc, à ce que je voi,
Que vous avez voulu me ramener chez moi ? 10

ALCESTE. Je ne querelle point ; mais votre humeur, madame,
Ouvre au premier venu trop d'accès dans votre âme :
Vous avez trop d'amants qu'on voit vous obséder,
Et mon cœur de cela ne peut s'accommoder. 15

CÉLIMÈNE. Des amants que je fais me rendez-vous coupable ?
Puis-je empêcher les gens de me trouver aimable ?
Et lorsque pour me voir ils font de doux efforts,
Dois-je prendre un bâton pour les mettre dehors ? 20

ALCESTE. Non, ce n'est pas, madame, un bâton qu'il faut prendre,
Mais un cœur à leurs vœux moins facile et moins tendre.
Je sais que vos appas vous suivent en tous lieux ;
Mais votre accueil retient ceux qu'attirent vos yeux : 25
Et sa douceur offerte à qui vous rend les armes,
Achève sur les cœurs l'ouvrage de vos charmes.

ALCESTE

*Je ne querelle point.*

Le trop riant espoir que vous leur présentez
Attache autour de vous leurs assiduités ;
Et votre complaisance un peu moins étendue
De tant de soupirants chasserait la cohue.
Mais au moins dites-moi, madame, par quel sort 5
Votre Clitandre a l'heur de vous plaire si fort ?
Sur quel fonds de mérite et de vertu sublime
Appuyez-vous en lui l'honneur de votre estime ?
Est-ce par l'ongle long qu'il porte au petit doigt
Qu'il s'est acquis chez vous l'estime où l'on le voit ? 10
Vous êtes-vous rendue, avec tout le beau monde,
Au mérite éclatant de sa perruque blonde ?
Sont-ce ses grands canons qui vous le font aimer ?
L'amas de ses rubans a-t-il su vous charmer ?
Est-ce par les appas de sa vaste rhingrave 15
Qu'il a gagné votre âme en faisant votre esclave ?
Ou sa façon de rire et son ton de fausset
Ont-ils de vous toucher su trouver le secret ?

CÉLIMÈNE. Qu'injustement de lui vous prenez de l'ombrage ! 20
Ne savez-vous pas bien pourquoi je le ménage,
Et que dans mon procès, ainsi qu'il m'a promis,
Il peut intéresser tout ce qu'il a d'amis ?

ALCESTE. Perdez votre procès, madame, avec constance,
Et ne ménagez point un rival qui m'offense. 25

CÉLIMÈNE. Mais de tout l'univers vous devenez jaloux.

ALCESTE. C'est que tout l'univers est bien reçu de vous.

CÉLIMÈNE. C'est ce qui doit rasseoir votre âme effarouchée,
Puisque ma complaisance est sur tous épanchée ;
Et vous auriez plus lieu de vous en offenser, 30
Si vous me la voyiez sur un seul ramasser.

ALCESTE. Mais moi, que vous blâmez de trop de jalousie,
Qu'ai-je de plus qu'eux tous, madame, je vous prie ?

CÉLIMÈNE. Le bonheur de savoir que vous êtes aimé.

ALCESTE. Et quel lieu de le croire a mon cœur enflammé ? 35

CÉLIMÈNE. Je pense qu'ayant pris le soin de vous le dire,
Un aveu de la sorte a de quoi vous suffire.

ALCESTE. Mais qui m'assurera que, dans le même instant,
Vous n'en disiez peut-être aux autres tout autant ?

CÉLIMÈNE. Certes, pour un amant, la fleurette est mignonne, 5
Et vous me traitez là de gentille personne.
Hé bien ! pour vous ôter d'un semblable souci,
De tout ce que j'ai dit je me dédis ici,
Et rien ne saurait plus vous tromper que vous-même : 10
Soyez content.

ALCESTE. Morbleu ! faut-il que je vous aime ?
Ah ! que si de vos mains je rattrape mon cœur,
Je bénirai le Ciel de ce rare bonheur !
Je ne le cèle pas, je fais tout mon possible 15
A rompre de ce cœur l'attachement terrible ;
Mais mes plus grands efforts n'ont rien fait jusqu'ici,
Et c'est pour mes péchés que je vous aime ainsi.

CÉLIMÈNE. Il est vrai, votre ardeur est pour moi sans seconde. 20

ALCESTE. Oui, je puis là-dessus défier tout le monde.
Mon amour ne se peut concevoir, et jamais
Personne n'a, madame, aimé comme je fais.

CÉLIMÈNE. En effet, la méthode en est toute nouvelle,
Car vous aimez les gens pour leur faire querelle ; 25
Ce n'est qu'en mots fâcheux qu'éclate votre ardeur,
Et l'on n'a vu jamais un amour si grondeur.

ALCESTE. Mais il ne tient qu'à vous que son chagrin ne passe.
A tous nos démêlés coupons chemin, de grâce, 30
Parlons à cœur ouvert, et voyons d'arrêter. . . .

## SCÈNE II

*Célimène, Alceste, Basque*

CÉLIMÈNE. Qu'est-ce ?
BASQUE. Acaste est là-bas.
CÉLIMÈNE. Hé bien ! faites monter.
ALCESTE. Quoi ? l'on ne peut jamais vous parler tête à tête ? 5
A recevoir le monde on vous voit toujours prête ?
Et vous ne pouvez pas, un seul moment de tous,
Vous résoudre à souffrir de n'être pas chez vous ?
CÉLIMÈNE. Voulez-vous qu'avec lui je me fasse une affaire ? 10
ALCESTE. Vous avez des regards qui ne sauraient me plaire.
CÉLIMÈNE. C'est un homme à jamais ne me le pardonner,
S'il savait que sa vue eût pu m'importuner.
ALCESTE. Et que vous fait cela, pour vous gêner de sorte . . . ? 15
CÉLIMÈNE. Mon Dieu ! de ses pareils la bienveillance importe ;
Et ce sont de ces gens qui, je ne sais comment,
Ont gagné dans la cour de parler hautement. 20
Dans tous les entretiens on les voit s'introduire ;
Ils ne sauraient servir, mais ils peuvent vous nuire ;
Et jamais, quelque appui qu'on puisse avoir d'ailleurs,
On ne doit se brouiller avec ces grands brailleurs.
ALCESTE. Enfin, quoi qu'il en soit, et sur quoi qu'on se fonde, 25
Vous trouvez des raisons pour souffrir tout le monde ;
Et les précautions de votre jugement. . . .

## SCÈNE III

*Basque, Alceste, Célimène*

BASQUE. Voici Clitandre encor, madame.
ALCESTE [*Il témoigne s'en vouloir aller*]. Justement.
CÉLIMÈNE. Où courez-vous ?
ALCESTE. Je sors.
CÉLIMÈNE. Demeurez. 5
ALCESTE. Pourquoi faire ?
CÉLIMÈNE. Demeurez.
ALCESTE. Je ne puis.
CÉLIMÈNE. Je le veux. 10
ALCESTE. Point d'affaire.
Ces conversations ne font que m'ennuyer,
Et c'est trop que vouloir me les faire essuyer.
CÉLIMÈNE. Je le veux, je le veux.
ALCESTE. Non, il m'est impossible. 15
CÉLIMÈNE. Hé bien ! allez, sortez, il vous est tout loisible

## SCÈNE IV

*Éliante, Philinte, Acaste, Clitandre, Alceste, Célimène, Basque*

ÉLIANTE. Voici les deux marquis qui montent avec nous :
Vous l'est-on venu dire ?
CÉLIMÈNE. Oui. Des sièges pour tous.
*A Alceste.*
Vous n'êtes pas sorti ? 20
ALCESTE. Non : Mais je veux, madame,
Ou pour eux, ou pour moi, faire expliquer votre âme.
CÉLIMÈNE. Taisez-vous.
ALCESTE. Aujourd'hui vous vous expliquerez.
CÉLIMÈNE. Vous perdez le sens. 25

ALCESTE. Point. Vous vous déclarerez.
CÉLIMÈNE. Ah !
ALCESTE. Vous prendrez parti.
CÉLIMÈNE. Vous vous moquez, je pense. 5
ALCESTE. Non ; mais vous choisirez ; c'est trop de patience.
CLITANDRE. Parbleu ! je viens du Louvre, où Cléonte, au levé, 10
Madame, a bien paru ridicule achevé.
N'a-t-il point quelque ami qui pût, sur ses manières,
D'un charitable avis lui prêter les lumières ?
CÉLIMÈNE. Dans le monde, à vrai dire, il se barbouille fort ;
Partout il porte un air qui saute aux yeux d'abord ; 15
Et lorsqu'on le revoit après un peu d'absence,
On le retrouve encor plus plein d'extravagance.
ACASTE. Parbleu ! s'il faut parler des gens extravagants,
Je viens d'en essuyer un des plus fatigants ;
Damon, le raisonneur, qui m'a, ne vous déplaise, 20
Une heure, au grand soleil, tenu hors de ma chaise.
CÉLIMÈNE. C'est un parleur étrange, et qui trouve toujours
L'art de ne vous rien dire avec de grands discours :
Dans les propos qu'il tient on ne voit jamais goutte,
Et ce n'est que du bruit que tout ce qu'on écoute. 25
ÉLIANTE, *à Philinte.* Ce début n'est pas mal ; et contre le prochain
La conversation prend un assez bon train.
CLITANDRE. Timante encor, madame, est un bon caractère.
CÉLIMÈNE. C'est de la tête aux pieds un homme tout mystère, 30
Qui vous jette en passant un coup d'œil égaré,
Et, sans aucune affaire, est toujours affairé.
Tout ce qu'il vous débite en grimaces abonde ;
A force de façons il assomme le monde ; 35

Sans cesse il a, tout bas, pour rompre l'entretien,
Un secret à vous dire, et ce secret n'est rien ;
De la moindre vétille il fait une merveille,
Et jusques au bonjour, il dit tout à l'oreille.

ACASTE. Et Géralde, madame ? 5

CÉLIMÈNE. O l'ennuyeux conteur !
Jamais on ne le voit sortir du grand seigneur;
Dans le brillant commerce il se mêle sans cesse,
Et ne cite jamais que duc, prince ou princesse :
La qualité l'entête ; et tous ses entretiens 10
Ne sont que de chevaux, d'équipage, et de chiens ;
Il tutoie en parlant ceux du plus haut étage,
Et le nom de monsieur est chez lui hors d'usage.

CLITANDRE. On dit qu'avec Bélise il est du dernier bien.

CÉLIMÈNE. Le pauvre esprit de femme, et le sec entretien ! 15
Lorsqu'elle vient me voir, je souffre le martyre ;
Il faut suer sans cesse à chercher que lui dire,
Et la stérilité de son expression
Fait mourir à tous coups la conversation.
En vain, pour attaquer son stupide silence, 20
De tous les lieux communs vous prenez l'assistance ;
Le beau temps et la pluie, et le froid et le chaud
Sont des fonds qu'avec elle on épuise bientôt.
Cependant sa visite, assez insupportable,
Traîne en une longueur encore épouvantable ; 25
Et l'on demande l'heure, et l'on bâille vingt fois,
Qu'elle grouille aussi peu qu'une pièce de bois.

ACASTE. Que vous semble d'Adraste ?

CÉLIMÈNE. Ah ! quel orgueil extrême ! 30
C'est un homme gonflé de l'amour de soi-même.
Son mérite jamais n'est content de la cour :
Contre elle il fait métier de pester chaque jour,
Et l'on ne donne emploi, charge ni bénéfice,
Qu'à tout ce qu'il se croit on ne fasse injustice. 35

CLITANDRE. Mais le jeune Cléon, chez qui vont aujourd'hui
Nos plus honnêtes gens, que dites-vous de lui ?
CÉLIMÈNE. Que de son cuisinier il s'est fait un mérite,
Et que c'est à sa table à qui l'on rend visite.
ÉLIANTE. Il prend soin d'y servir des mets fort délicats. 5
CÉLIMÈNE. Oui ; mais je voudrais bien qu'il ne s'y servît pas ;
C'est un fort méchant plat que sa sotte personne,
Et qui gâte, à mon goût, tous les repas qu'il donne.
PHILINTE. On fait assez de cas de son oncle Damis ; 10
Qu'en dites-vous, madame ?
CÉLIMÈNE. Il est de mes amis.
PHILINTE. Je le trouve honnête homme, et d'un air assez sage.
CÉLIMÈNE. Oui ; mais il veut avoir trop d'esprit, dont j'enrage ; 15
Il est guindé sans cesse ; et dans tous ses propos,
On voit qu'il se travaille à dire de bons mots.
Depuis que dans la tête il s'est mis d'être habile,
Rien ne touche son goût, tant il est difficile ; 20
Il veut voir des défauts à tout ce qu'on écrit,
Et pense que louer n'est pas d'un bel esprit,
Que c'est être savant que trouver à redire,
Qu'il n'appartient qu'aux sots d'admirer et de rire,
Et qu'en n'approuvant rien des ouvrages du temps, 25
Il se met au-dessus de tous les autres gens ;
Aux conversations même il trouve à reprendre :
Ce sont propos trop bas pour y daigner descendre ;
Et, les deux bras croisés, du haut de son esprit
Il regarde en pitié tout ce que chacun dit. 30
ACASTE. Dieu me damne, voilà son portrait véritable.
CLITANDRE. Pour bien peindre les gens vous êtes admirable.
ALCESTE. Allons, ferme, poussez, mes bons amis de cour ;
Vous n'en épargnez point, et chacun a son tour : 35

Cependant aucun d'eux à vos yeux ne se montre,
Qu'on ne vous voie, en hâte, aller à sa rencontre,
Lui présenter la main, et d'un baiser flatteur
Appuyer les serments d'être son serviteur.

CLITANDRE. Pourquoi s'en prendre à nous ? Si ce qu'on dit vous blesse, 5
Il faut que le reproche à madame s'adresse.

ALCESTE. Non, morbleu ! c'est à vous ; et vos ris complaisants
Tirent de son esprit tous ces traits médisants. 10
Son humeur satirique est sans cesse nourrie
Par le coupable encens de votre flatterie ;
Et son cœur à railler trouverait moins d'appas,
S'il avait observé qu'on ne l'applaudît pas.
C'est ainsi qu'aux flatteurs on doit partout se prendre 15
Des vices où l'on voit les humains se répandre.

PHILINTE. Mais pourquoi pour ces gens un intérêt si grand,
Vous qui condamneriez ce qu'en eux on reprend ?

CÉLIMÈNE. Et ne faut-il pas bien que monsieur contredise ? 20
A la commune voix veut-on qu'il se réduise,
Et qu'il ne fasse pas éclater en tous lieux
L'esprit contrariant qu'il a reçu des cieux ?
Le sentiment d'autrui n'est jamais pour lui plaire ;
Il prend toujours en main l'opinion contraire, 25
Et penserait paraître un homme du commun,
Si l'on voyait qu'il fût de l'avis de quelqu'un.
L'honneur de contredire a pour lui tant de charmes,
Qu'il prend contre lui-même assez souvent les armes ;
Et ses vrais sentiments sont combattus par lui, 30
Aussitôt qu'il les voit dans la bouche d'autrui.

ALCESTE. Les rieurs sont pour vous, madame, c'est tout dire,
Et vous pouvez pousser contre moi la satire.

PHILINTE. Mais il est véritable aussi que votre esprit 35

Se gendarme toujours contre tout ce qu'on dit,
Et que, par un chagrin que lui-même il avoue,
Il ne saurait souffrir qu'on blâme, ni qu'on loue.

ALCESTE. C'est que jamais, morbleu ! les hommes n'ont raison, 5
Que le chagrin contre eux est toujours de saison,
Et que je vois qu'ils sont, sur toutes les affaires,
Loueurs impertinents, ou censeurs téméraires.

CÉLIMÈNE. Mais. . . .

ALCESTE. Non, madame, non ; quand j'en devrais mourir, 10
Vous avez des plaisirs que je ne puis souffrir ;
Et l'on a tort ici de nourrir dans votre âme
Ce grand attachement aux défauts qu'on y blâme.

CLITANDRE. Pour moi, je ne sais pas, mais j'avouerai tout haut 15
Que j'ai cru jusqu'ici madame sans défaut.

ACASTE. De grâces et d'attraits je vois qu'elle est pourvue ;
Mais les défauts qu'elle a ne frappent point ma vue.

ALCESTE. Ils frappent tous la mienne ; et loin de m'en cacher, 20
Elle sait que j'ai soin de les lui reprocher.
Plus on aime quelqu'un, moins il faut qu'on le flatte ;
A ne rien pardonner le pur amour éclate ;
Et je bannirais, moi, tous ces lâches amants 25
Que je verrais soumis à tous mes sentiments,
Et dont, à tout propos, les molles complaisances
Donneraient de l'encens à mes extravagances.

CÉLIMÈNE. Enfin, s'il faut qu'à vous s'en rapportent les cœurs, 30
On doit, pour bien aimer, renoncer aux douceurs,
Et du parfait amour mettre l'honneur suprême
A bien injurier les personnes qu'on aime.

ÉLIANTE. L'amour, pour l'ordinaire, est peu fait à ces lois,
Et l'on voit les amants vanter toujours leur choix ; 35

Jamais leur passion n'y voit rien de blâmable,
Et dans l'objet aimé tout leur devient aimable ;
Ils comptent les défauts pour des perfections,
Et savent y donner de favorables noms.
La pâle est aux jasmins en blancheur comparable ; 5
La noire à faire peur, une brune adorable ;
La maigre a de la taille et de la liberté ;
La grasse est dans son port pleine de majesté ;
La malpropre sur soi, de peu d'attraits chargée,
Est mise sous le nom de beauté négligée ; 10
La géante paraît une déesse aux yeux ;
La naine, un abrégé des merveilles des cieux ;
L'orgueilleuse a le cœur digne d'une couronne ;
La fourbe a de l'esprit ; la sotte est toute bonne ;
La trop grande parleuse est d'agréable humeur ; 15
Et la muette garde une honnête pudeur.
C'est ainsi qu'un amant dont l'ardeur est extrême
Aime jusqu'aux défauts des personnes qu'il aime.

ALCESTE. Et moi, je soutiens, moi . . .

CÉLIMÈNE. Brisons là ce discours, 20
Et dans la galerie allons faire deux tours.
Quoi ? vous vous en allez, messieurs ?

CLITANDRE et ACASTE. Non pas, madame.

ALCESTE. La peur de leur départ occupe fort votre âme.
Sortez quand vous voudrez, messieurs ; mais j'avertis 25
Que je ne sors qu'après que vous serez sortis.

ACASTE. A moins de voir madame en être importunée,
Rien ne m'appelle ailleurs de toute la journée.

CLITANDRE. Moi, pourvu que je puisse être au petit
couché, 30
Je n'ai point d'autre affaire où je sois attaché.

CÉLIMÈNE. C'est pour rire, je crois.

ALCESTE. Non, en aucune sorte :
Nous verrons si c'est moi que vous voudrez qui sorte.

## SCÈNE V

*Basque, Alceste, Célimène, Éliante, Acaste, Philinte, Clitandre*

BASQUE. Monsieur, un homme est là qui voudrait vous parler,
Pour affaire, dit-il, qu'on ne peut reculer.
ALCESTE. Dis-lui que je n'ai point d'affaires si pressées.
BASQUE. Il porte une jaquette à grand'basques plissées, 5
Avec du dor dessus.
CÉLIMÈNE. Allez voir ce que c'est,
Ou bien faites-le entrer.
ALCESTE. Qu'est-ce donc qu'il vous plaît?
Venez, monsieur. 10

## SCÈNE VI

*Garde, Alceste, Célimène, Éliante, Acaste, Philinte, Clitandre*

GARDE. Monsieur, j'ai deux mots à vous dire.
ALCESTE. Vous pouvez parler haut, monsieur, pour m'en instruire.
GARDE. Messieurs les Maréchaux, dont j'ai commandement, 15
Vous mandent de venir les trouver promptement,
Monsieur.
ALCESTE. Qui? moi, monsieur?
GARDE. Vous-même.
ALCESTE. Et pourquoi faire? 20
PHILINTE. C'est d'Oronte et de vous la ridicule affaire.
CÉLIMÈNE. Comment?
PHILINTE. Oronte et lui se sont tantôt bravés
Sur certains petits vers qu'il n'a pas approuvés; 25
Et l'on veut assoupir la chose en sa naissance.

ALCESTE. Moi, je n'aurai jamais de lâche complaisance.
PHILINTE. Mais il faut suivre l'ordre : allons, disposez-
 vous. . . .
ALCESTE. Quel accommodement veut-on faire entre nous ?
 La voix de ces messieurs me condamnera-t-elle 5
 A trouver bons les vers qui font notre querelle ?
 Je ne me dédis point de ce que j'en ai dit,
 Je les trouve méchants.
PHILINTE. Mais d'un plus doux esprit. . . .
ALCESTE. Je n'en démordrai point : les vers sont exécrables. 10
PHILINTE. Vous devez faire voir des sentiments traitables.
 Allons, venez.
ALCESTE. J'irai ; mais rien n'aura pouvoir
 De me faire dédire.
PHILINTE. Allons vous faire voir. 15
ALCESTE. Hors qu'un commandement exprès du Roi me
 vienne,
 De trouver bons les vers dont on se met en peine,
 Je soutiendrai toujours, morbleu ! qu'ils sont mauvais,
 Et qu'un homme est pendable après les avoir faits. 20
*A Clitandre et Acaste, qui rient.*
 Par le sangbleu ! messieurs, je ne croyais pas être
 Si plaisant que je suis.
CÉLIMÈNE. Allez vite paraître
 Où vous devez. 25
ALCESTE. J'y vais, madame, et sur mes pas
 Je reviens en ce lieu, pour vider nos débats.

# ACTE III

## SCÈNE PREMIÈRE

*Clitandre, Acaste*

CLITANDRE. Cher marquis, je te vois l'âme bien satisfaite ;
Toute chose t'égaye, et rien ne t'inquiète.
En bonne foi, crois-tu, sans t'éblouir les yeux,
Avoir de grands sujets de paraître joyeux ?

ACASTE. Parbleu ! je ne vois pas, lorsque je m'examine, 5
Où prendre aucun sujet d'avoir l'âme chagrine.
J'ai du bien, je suis jeune, et sors d'une maison
Qui se peut dire noble avec quelque raison ;
Et je crois, par le rang que me donne ma race,
Qu'il est fort peu d'emplois dont je ne sois en passe. 10
Pour le cœur, dont sur tout nous devons faire cas,
On sait, sans vanité, que je n'en manque pas,
Et l'on m'a vu pousser, dans le monde, une affaire
D'une assez vigoureuse et gaillarde manière.
Pour de l'esprit, j'en ai sans doute, et du bon goût 15
A juger sans étude et raisonner de tout,
A faire aux nouveautés, dont je suis idolâtre,
Figure de savant sur les bancs du théâtre,
Y décider en chef, et faire du fracas
A tous les beaux endroits qui méritent des has. 20
Je suis assez adroit ; j'ai bon air, bonne mine,
Les dents belles surtout, et la taille fort fine.
Quant à se mettre bien, je crois, sans me flatter,
Qu'on serait mal venu de me le disputer.
Je me vois dans l'estime autant qu'on y puisse être, 25
Fort aimé du beau sexe, et bien auprès du maître.
Je crois qu'avec cela, mon cher marquis, je croi
Qu'on peut, par tout pays, être content de soi.

CLITANDRE. Oui ; mais, trouvant ailleurs des conquêtes
faciles,
Pourquoi pousser ici des soupirs inutiles ?
ACASTE. Moi ? Parbleu ! je ne suis de taille ni d'humeur
A pouvoir d'une belle essuyer la froideur. 5
C'est aux gens mal tournés, aux mérites vulgaires,
A brûler constamment pour des beautés sévères,
A languir à leurs pieds et souffrir leurs rigueurs,
A chercher le secours des soupirs et des pleurs,
Et tâcher, par des soins d'une très longue suite, 10
D'obtenir ce qu'on nie à leur peu de mérite.
Mais les gens de mon air, marquis, ne sont pas faits
Pour aimer à crédit, et faire tous les frais.
Quelque rare que soit le mérite des belles,
Je pense, Dieu merci ! qu'on vaut son prix comme elles, 15
Que pour se faire honneur d'un cœur comme le mien,
Ce n'est pas la raison qu'il ne leur coûte rien,
Et qu'au moins, à tout mettre en de justes balances,
Il faut qu'à frais communs se fassent les avances.
CLITANDRE. Tu penses donc, marquis, être fort bien ici ? 20
ACASTE. J'ai quelque lieu, marquis, de le penser ainsi.
CLITANDRE. Crois-moi, détache-toi de cette erreur extrême :
Tu te flattes, mon cher, et t'aveugles toi-même.
ACASTE. Il est vrai, je me flatte et m'aveugle en effet.
CLITANDRE. Mais qui te fait juger ton bonheur si parfait ? 25
ACASTE. Je me flatte.
CLITANDRE. Sur quoi fonder tes conjectures ?
ACASTE. Je m'aveugle.
CLITANDRE. En as-tu des preuves qui soient
sûres ? 30
ACASTE. Je m'abuse, te dis-je.
CLITANDRE. Est-ce que de ses vœux
Célimène t'a fait quelques secrets aveux ?
ACASTE. Non, je suis maltraité.
CLITANDRE. Réponds-moi, je te prie. 35

ACASTE. Je n'ai que des rebuts.

CLITANDRE. Laissons la raillerie,
Et me dis quel espoir on peut t'avoir donné.

ACASTE. Je suis le misérable, et toi le fortuné :
On a pour ma personne une aversion grande, 5
Et quelqu'un de ces jours il faut que je me pende.

CLITANDRE. O ! çà, veux-tu, marquis, pour ajuster nos vœux,
Que nous tombions d'accord d'une chose tous deux ?
Que, qui pourra montrer une marque certaine 10
D'avoir meilleure part au cœur de Célimène,
L'autre ici fera place au vainqueur prétendu,
Et le délivrera d'un rival assidu ?

ACASTE. Ah, parbleu ! tu me plais avec un tel langage,
Et du bon de mon cœur à cela je m'engage. 15
Mais, chut !

## SCÈNE II

*Célimène, Acaste, Clitandre*

CÉLIMÈNE. Encore ici ?

CLITANDRE. L'amour retient nos pas.

CÉLIMÈNE. Je viens d'ouïr entrer un carrosse là-bas :
Savez-vous qui c'est ? 20

CLITANDRE. Non.

## SCÈNE III

*Basque, Célimène, Acaste, Clitandre*

BASQUE. Arsinoé, madame,
Monte ici pour vous voir.

CÉLIMÈNE Que me veut cette femme ?

**CLITANDRE**

*Laissons la raillerie.*

BASQUE. Éliante là-bas est à l'entretenir.
CÉLIMÈNE. De quoi s'avise-t-elle, et qui la fait venir ?
ACASTE. Pour prude consommée en tous lieux elle passe,
Et l'ardeur de son zèle. . . .
CÉLIMÈNE. Oui, oui, franche grimace : 5
Dans l'âme elle est du monde, et ses soins tentent tout
Pour accrocher quelqu'un, sans en venir à bout.
Elle ne saurait voir qu'avec un œil d'envie
Les amants déclarés dont une autre est suivie ;
Et son triste mérite, abandonné de tous, 10
Contre le siècle aveugle est toujours en courroux.
Elle tâche à couvrir d'un faux voile de prude
Ce que chez elle on voit d'affreuse solitude ;
Et pour sauver l'honneur de ses faibles appas,
Elle attache du crime au pouvoir qu'ils n'ont pas. 15
Cependant un amant plairait fort à la dame,
Et même pour Alceste elle a tendresse d'âme.
Ce qu'il me rend de soins outrage ses attraits,
Elle veut que ce soit un vol que je lui fais ;
Et son jaloux dépit, qu'avec peine elle cache, 20
En tous endroits, sous main, contre moi se détache.
Enfin je n'ai rien vu de si sot à mon gré,
Elle est impertinente au suprême degré,
Et . . .

## SCÈNE IV

*Arsinoé, Célimène*

CÉLIMÈNE. Ah ! quel heureux sort en ce lieu vous amène ? 25
Madame, sans mentir, j'étais de vous en peine.
ARSINOÉ. Je viens pour quelque avis que j'ai cru vous devoir.
CÉLIMÈNE. Ah ! mon Dieu ! que je suis contente de vous voir ! 30

ARSINOÉ. Leur départ ne pouvait plus à propos se faire.
CÉLIMÈNE. Voulons-nous nous asseoir?
ARSINOÉ. Il n'est pas nécessaire,
Madame. L'amitié doit surtout éclater
Aux choses qui le plus nous peuvent importer ; 5
Et comme il n'en est point de plus grande importance
Que celles de l'honneur et de la bienséance,
Je viens, par un avis qui touche votre honneur,
Témoigner l'amitié que pour vous a mon cœur.
Hier j'étais chez des gens de vertu singulière, 10
Où sur vous du discours on tourna la matière ;
Et là, votre conduite, avec ses grands éclats,
Madame, eut le malheur qu'on ne la loua pas.
Cette foule de gens dont vous souffrez visite,
Votre galanterie, et les bruits qu'elle excite 15
Trouvèrent des censeurs plus qu'il n'aurait fallu,
Et bien plus rigoureux que je n'eusse voulu.
Vous pouvez bien penser quel parti je sus prendre ;
Je fis ce que je pus pour vous pouvoir défendre,
Je vous excusai fort sur votre intention, 20
Et voulus de votre âme être la caution.
Mais vous savez qu'il est des choses dans la vie
Qu'on ne peut excuser, quoiqu'on en ait envie ;
Et je me vis contrainte à demeurer d'accord
Que l'air dont vous viviez vous faisait un peu tort, 25
Qu'il prenait dans le monde une méchante face,
Qu'il n'est conte fâcheux que partout on n'en fasse,
Et que, si vous vouliez, tous vos déportements
Pourraient moins donner prise aux mauvais jugements.
Non que j'y croie, au fond, l'honnêteté blessée ; 30
Me préserve le Ciel d'en avoir la pensée !
Mais aux ombres du crime on prête aisément foi,
Et ce n'est pas assez de bien vivre pour soi.
Madame, je vous crois l'âme trop raisonnable,
Pour ne pas prendre bien cet avis profitable, 35

Et pour l'attribuer qu'aux mouvements secrets
D'un zèle qui m'attache à tous vos intérêts.

CÉLIMÈNE. Madame, j'ai beaucoup de grâces à vous rendre ;
Un tel avis m'oblige, et loin de le mal prendre, 5
J'en prétends reconnaître, à l'instant, la faveur,
Par un avis aussi qui touche votre honneur ;
Et comme je vous vois vous montrer mon amie,
En m'apprenant les bruits que de moi l'on publie,
Je veux suivre, à mon tour, un exemple si doux, 10
En vous avertissant de ce qu'on dit de vous.
En un lieu, l'autre jour, où je faisais visite,
Je trouvai quelques gens d'un très rare mérite,
Qui, parlant des vrais soins d'une âme qui vit bien,
Firent tomber sur vous, madame, l'entretien. 15
Là, votre pruderie et vos éclats de zèle
Ne furent pas cités comme un fort bon modèle :
Cette affectation d'un grave extérieur,
Vos discours éternels de sagesse et d'honneur,
Vos mines et vos cris aux ombres d'indécence 20
Que d'un mot ambigu peut avoir l'innocence,
Cette hauteur d'estime où vous êtes de vous,
Et ces yeux de pitié que vous jetez sur tous,
Vos fréquentes leçons et vos aigres censures
Sur des choses qui sont innocentes et pures, 25
Tout cela, si je puis vous parler franchement,
Madame, fut blâmé d'un commun sentiment.
A quoi bon, disaient-ils, cette mine modeste,
Et ce sage dehors que dément tout le reste ?
Elle est à bien prier exacte au dernier point ; 30
Mais elle bat ses gens, et ne les paye point.
Dans tous les lieux dévots elle étale un grand zèle ;
Mais elle met du blanc, et veut paraître belle.
Elle fait des tableaux couvrir les nudités ;
Mais elle a de l'amour pour les réalités. 35

Pour moi, contre chacun je pris votre défense,
Et leur assurai fort que c'était médisance ;
Mais tous les sentiments combattirent le mien ;
Et leur conclusion fut que vous feriez bien
De prendre moins de soin des actions des autres, 5
Et de vous mettre un peu plus en peine des vôtres ;
Qu'on doit se regarder soi-même un fort long temps
Avant que de songer à condamner les gens ;
Qu'il faut mettre le poids d'une vie exemplaire
Dans les corrections qu'aux autres on veut faire ; 10
Et qu'encor vaut-il mieux s'en remettre, au besoin,
A ceux à qui le Ciel en a commis le soin.
Madame, je vous crois aussi trop raisonnable
Pour ne pas prendre bien cet avis profitable,
Et pour l'attribuer qu'aux mouvements secrets 15
D'un zèle qui m'attache à tous vos intérêts.

ARSINOÉ. A quoi qu'en reprenant on soit assujettie,
Je ne m'attendais pas à cette repartie,
Madame, et je vois bien, par ce qu'elle a d'aigreur,
Que mon sincère avis vous a blessée au cœur. 20

CÉLIMÈNE. Au contraire, madame ; et, si l'on était sage,
Ces avis mutuels seraient mis en usage :
On détruirait par là, traitant de bonne foi,
Ce grand aveuglement où chacun est pour soi.
Il ne tiendra qu'à vous qu'avec le même zèle 25
Nous ne continuions cet office fidèle,
Et ne prenions grand soin de nous dire, entre nous,
Ce que nous entendrons, vous de moi, moi de vous.

ARSINOÉ. Ah ! madame, de vous je ne puis rien entendre ;
C'est en moi que l'on peut trouver fort à reprendre. 30

CÉLIMÈNE. Madame, on peut, je crois, louer et blâmer tout,
Et chacun a raison suivant l'âge ou le goût.
Il est une saison pour la galanterie ;
Il en est une aussi propre à la pruderie.
On peut, par politique, en prendre le parti, 35

Quand de nos jeunes ans l'éclat est amorti :
Cela sert à couvrir de fâcheuses disgrâces.
Je ne dis pas qu'un jour je ne suive vos traces ;
L'âge amènera tout, et ce n'est pas le temps,
Madame, comme on sait, d'être prude à vingt ans. 5

ARSINOÉ. Certes, vous vous targuez d'un bien faible avantage,
Et vous faites sonner terriblement votre âge.
Ce que de plus que vous on en pourrait avoir
N'est pas un si grand cas pour s'en tant prévaloir ; 10
Et je ne sais pourquoi votre âme ainsi s'emporte,
Madame, à me pousser de cette étrange sorte.

CÉLIMÈNE. Et moi, je ne sais pas, madame, aussi pourquoi
On vous voit, en tous lieux, vous déchaîner sur moi.
Faut-il de vos chagrins, sans cesse, à moi vous prendre ? 15
Et puis-je mais des soins qu'on ne va pas vous rendre ?
Si ma personne aux gens inspire de l'amour,
Et si l'on continue à m'offrir chaque jour
Des vœux que votre cœur peut souhaiter qu'on m'ôte,
Je n'y saurais que faire, et ce n'est pas ma faute ; 20
Vous avez le champ libre, et je n'empêche pas
Que pour les attirer vous n'ayez des appas.

ARSINOÉ. Hélas ! et croyez-vous que l'on se mette en peine
De ce nombre d'amants dont vous faites la vaine,
Et qu'il ne nous soit pas fort aisé de juger 25
A quel prix aujourd'hui l'on peut les engager ?
Pensez-vous faire croire, à voir comme tout roule,
Que votre seul mérite attire cette foule ?
Qu'ils ne brûlent pour vous que d'un honnête amour,
Et que pour vos vertus ils vous font tous la cour ? 30
On ne s'aveugle point par de vaines défaites,
Le monde n'est point dupe ; et j'en vois qui sont faites
A pouvoir inspirer de tendres sentiments,
Qui chez elles pourtant ne fixent point d'amants ;
Et de là nous pouvons tirer des conséquences, 35

Qu'on n'acquiert point leurs cœurs sans de grandes
avances,
Qu'aucun pour nos beaux yeux n'est notre soupirant,
Et qu'il faut acheter tous les soins qu'on nous rend.
Ne vous enflez donc point d'une si grande gloire 5
Pour les petits brillants d'une faible victoire ;
Et corrigez un peu l'orgueil de vos appas,
De traiter pour cela les gens de haut en bas.
Si nos yeux enviaient les conquêtes des vôtres,
Je pense qu'on pourrait faire comme les autres, 10
Ne se point ménager, et vous faire bien voir
Que l'on a des amants quand on en veut avoir.

CÉLIMÈNE. Ayez-en donc, madame, et voyons cette affaire ;
Par ce rare secret efforcez-vous de plaire ;
Et sans. . . . 15

ARSINOÉ. Brisons, madame, un pareil entretien ;
Il pousserait trop loin votre esprit et le mien ;
Et j'aurais pris déjà le congé qu'il faut prendre,
Si mon carrosse encor ne m'obligeait d'attendre.

CÉLIMÈNE. Autant qu'il vous plaira vous pouvez arrêter, 20
Madame, et là-dessus rien ne doit vous hâter ;
Mais, sans vous fatiguer de ma cérémonie,
Je m'en vais vous donner meilleure compagnie ;
Et monsieur, qu'à propos le hasard fait venir,
Remplira mieux ma place à vous entretenir. 25
Alceste, il faut que j'aille écrire un mot de lettre,
Que, sans me faire tort, je ne saurais remettre.
Soyez avec madame ; elle aura la bonté
D'excuser aisément mon incivilité.

## SCÈNE V

*Alceste, Arsinoé*

ARSINOÉ. Vous voyez, elle veut que je vous entretienne, 30
Attendant un moment que mon carrosse vienne ;

Et jamais tous ses soins ne pouvaient m'offrir rien
Qui me fût plus charmant qu'un pareil entretien.
En vérité, les gens d'un mérite sublime
Entraînent de chacun et l'amour et l'estime ;
Et le vôtre, sans doute, a des charmes secrets 5
Qui font entrer mon cœur dans tous vos intérêts.
Je voudrais que la cour, par un regard propice,
A ce que vous valez rendît plus de justice ;
Vous avez à vous plaindre, et je suis en courroux,
Quand je vois chaque jour qu'on ne fait rien pour vous. 10

ALCESTE. Moi, madame ! Et sur quoi pourrais-je en rien prétendre ?
Quel service à l'État est-ce qu'on m'a vu rendre ?
Qu'ai-je fait, s'il vous plaît, de si brillant de soi,
Pour me plaindre à la cour qu'on ne fait rien pour moi ? 15

ARSINOÉ. Tous ceux sur qui la cour jette des yeux propices,
N'ont pas toujours rendu de ces fameux services.
Il faut l'occasion, ainsi que le pouvoir ;
Et le mérite enfin que vous nous faites voir
Devrait. . . . 20

ALCESTE. Mon Dieu ! laissons mon mérite, de grâce ;
De quoi voulez-vous là que la cour s'embarrasse ?
Elle aurait fort à faire, et ses soins seraient grands
D'avoir à déterrer le mérite des gens.

ARSINOÉ. Un mérite éclatant se déterre lui-même : 25
Du vôtre, en bien des lieux, on fait un cas extrême ;
Et vous saurez de moi qu'en deux fort bons endroits
Vous fûtes hier loué par des gens d'un grand poids.

ALCESTE. Eh ! madame, l'on loue aujourd'hui tout le monde, 30
Et le siècle par là n'a rien qu'on ne confonde :
Tout est d'un grand mérite également doué,
Ce n'est plus un honneur que de se voir loué ;
D'éloges on regorge, à la tête on les jette,
Et mon valet de chambre est mis dans la Gazette. 35

ARSINOÉ. Pour moi, je voudrais bien que, pour vous montrer mieux,
Une charge à la cour vous pût frapper les yeux.
Pour peu que d'y songer vous nous fassiez les mines,
On peut pour vous servir remuer des machines, 5
Et j'ai des gens en main que j'emploierai pour vous,
Qui vous feront à tout un chemin assez doux.

ALCESTE. Et que voudriez-vous, madame, que j'y fisse ?
L'humeur dont je me sens veut que je m'en bannisse.
Le Ciel ne m'a point fait, en me donnant le jour, 10
Une âme compatible avec l'air de la cour ;
Je ne me trouve point les vertus nécessaires
Pour y bien réussir et faire mes affaires.
Être franc et sincère est mon plus grand talent ;
Je ne sais point jouer les hommes en parlant ; 15
Et qui n'a pas le don de cacher ce qu'il pense
Doit faire en ce pays fort peu de résidence.
Hors de la cour, sans doute, on n'a pas cet appui,
Et ces titres d'honneur qu'elle donne aujourd'hui ;
Mais on n'a pas aussi, perdant ces avantages, 20
Le chagrin de jouer de fort sots personnages ;
On n'a point à souffrir mille rebuts cruels,
On n'a point à louer les vers de messieurs tels,
A donner de l'encens à madame une telle,
Et de nos francs marquis essuyer la cervelle. 25

ARSINOÉ. Laissons, puisqu'il vous plaît, ce chapitre de cour :
Mais il faut que mon cœur vous plaigne en votre amour ;
Et pour vous découvrir là-dessus mes pensées,
Je souhaiterais fort vos ardeurs mieux placées. 30
Vous méritez, sans doute, un sort beaucoup plus doux,
Et celle qui vous charme est indigne de vous.

ALCESTE. Mais en disant cela, songez-vous, je vous prie,
Que cette personne est, madame, votre amie ?

ARSINOÉ. Oui ; mais ma conscience est blessée en effet 35

De souffrir plus longtemps le tort que l'on vous fait ;
L'état où je vous vois afflige trop mon âme,
Et je vous donne avis qu'on trahit votre flamme.
ALCESTE. C'est me montrer, madame, un tendre mouvement,
Et de pareils avis obligent un amant. 5
ARSINOÉ. Oui, toute mon amie, elle est et je la nomme
Indigne d'asservir le cœur d'un galant homme ;
Et le sien n'a pour vous que de feintes douceurs.
ALCESTE. Cela se peut, madame : on ne voit pas les cœurs ; 10
Mais votre charité se serait bien passée
De jeter dans le mien une telle pensée.
ARSINOÉ. Si vous ne voulez pas être désabusé,
Il faut ne vous rien dire, il est assez aisé.
ALCESTE. Non ; mais sur ce sujet, quoi que l'on nous expose, 15
Les doutes sont fâcheux plus que toute autre chose ;
Et je voudrais, pour moi, qu'on ne me fît savoir
Que ce qu'avec clarté l'on peut me faire voir.
ARSINOÉ. Hé bien ! c'est assez dit ; et sur cette matière 20
Vous allez recevoir une pleine lumière.
Oui, je veux que de tout vos yeux vous fassent foi ;
Donnez-moi seulement la main jusque chez moi ;
Là je vous ferai voir une preuve fidèle
De l'infidélité du cœur de votre belle ; 25
Et si pour d'autres yeux le vôtre peut brûler,
On pourra vous offrir de quoi vous consoler.

# ACTE IV

## SCÈNE PREMIÈRE

*Éliante, Philinte*

PHILINTE. Non, l'on n'a point vu d'âme à manier si dure,
Ni d'accommodement plus pénible à conclure ;
En vain de tous côtés on l'a voulu tourner,
Hors de son sentiment on n'a pu l'entraîner ;
Et jamais différend si bizarre, je pense, 5
N'avait de ces messieurs occupé la prudence.
« Non, messieurs, disait-il, je ne me dédis point,
Et tomberai d'accord de tout, hors de ce point.
De quoi s'offense-t-il ? et que veut-il me dire ?
Y va-t-il de sa gloire à ne pas bien écrire ? 10
Que lui fait mon avis, qu'il a pris de travers ?
On peut être honnête homme et faire mal des vers ;
Ce n'est point à l'honneur que touchent ces matières ;
Je le tiens galant homme en toutes les manières,
Homme de qualité, de mérite, et de cœur, 15
Tout ce qu'il vous plaira, mais fort méchant auteur.
Je louerai, si l'on veut, son train et sa dépense,
Son adresse à cheval, aux armes, à la danse ;
Mais, pour louer ses vers, je suis son serviteur ;
Et lorsque d'en mieux faire on n'a pas le bonheur, 20
On ne doit de rimer avoir aucune envie,
Qu'on n'y soit condamné sur peine de la vie. »
Enfin toute la grâce et l'accommodement
Où s'est, avec effort, plié son sentiment,
C'est de dire, croyant adoucir bien son style : 25
« Monsieur, je suis fâché d'être si difficile,
Et pour l'amour de vous, je voudrais, de bon cœur,

Avoir trouvé tantôt votre sonnet meilleur.»
Et dans une embrassade, on leur a, pour conclure,
Fait vite envelopper toute la procédure.

ÉLIANTE. Dans ses façons d'agir il est fort singulier ;
Mais j'en fais, je l'avoue, un cas particulier, 5
Et la sincérité dont son âme se pique
A quelque chose en soi de noble et d'héroïque.
C'est une vertu rare au siècle d'aujourd'hui,
Et je la voudrais voir partout comme chez lui.

PHILINTE. Pour moi, plus je le vois, plus surtout je m'étonne 10
De cette passion où son cœur s'abandonne :
De l'humeur dont le Ciel a voulu le former,
Je ne sais pas comment il s'avise d'aimer ;
Et je sais moins encor comment votre cousine 15
Peut être la personne où son penchant l'incline.

ÉLIANTE. Cela fait assez voir que l'amour, dans les cœurs,
N'est pas toujours produit par un rapport d'humeurs :
Et toutes ces raisons de douces sympathies
Dans cet exemple-ci se trouvent démenties. 20

PHILINTE. Mais croyez-vous qu'on l'aime, aux choses qu'on peut voir ?

ÉLIANTE. C'est un point qu'il n'est pas fort aisé de savoir.
Comment pouvoir juger s'il est vrai qu'elle l'aime ?
Son cœur de ce qu'il sent n'est pas bien sûr lui-même ; 25
Il aime quelquefois sans qu'il le sache bien,
Et croit aimer aussi parfois qu'il n'en est rien.

PHILINTE. Je crois que notre ami, près de cette cousine,
Trouvera des chagrins plus qu'il ne s'imagine ;
Et s'il avait mon cœur, à dire vérité, 30
Il tournerait ses vœux tout d'un autre côté,
Et par un choix plus juste, on le verrait, madame,
Profiter des bontés que lui montre votre âme.

ÉLIANTE. Pour moi, je n'en fais point de façons, et je croi
Qu'on doit, sur de tels points, être de bonne foi : 35

Je ne m'oppose point à toute sa tendresse ;
Au contraire, mon cœur pour elle s'intéresse ;
Et si c'était qu'à moi la chose pût tenir,
Moi-même à ce qu'il aime on me verrait l'unir.
Mais si dans un tel choix, comme tout se peut faire, 5
Son amour éprouvait quelque destin contraire,
S'il fallait que d'un autre on couronnât les feux,
Je pourrais me résoudre à recevoir ses vœux ;
Et le refus souffert, en pareille occurrence,
Ne m'y ferait trouver aucune répugnance. 10

PHILINTE. Et moi, de mon côté, je ne m'oppose pas,
Madame, à ces bontés qu'ont pour lui vos appas ;
Et lui-même, s'il veut, il peut bien vous instruire
De ce que là-dessus j'ai pris soin de lui dire.
Mais si, par un hymen qui les joindrait eux deux, 15
Vous étiez hors d'état de recevoir ses vœux,
Tous les miens tenteraient la faveur éclatante
Qu'avec tant de bonté votre âme lui présente :
Heureux si, quand son cœur s'y pourra dérober,
Elle pouvait sur moi, madame, retomber. 20

ÉLIANTE. Vous vous divertissez, Philinte.

PHILINTE. Non, madame,
Et je vous parle ici du meilleur de mon âme.
J'attends l'occasion de m'offrir hautement,
Et de tous mes souhaits j'en presse le moment. 25

## SCÈNE II

*Alceste, Éliante, Philinte*

ALCESTE. Ah ! faites-moi raison, madame, d'une offense
Qui vient de triompher de toute ma constance.

ÉLIANTE. Qu'est-ce donc ? Qu'avez-vous qui vous puisse émouvoir ?

ALCESTE. J'ai ce que sans mourir je ne puis concevoir ; 30

Et le déchaînement de toute la nature
Ne m'accablerait pas comme cette aventure.
C'en est fait. . . . Mon amour. . . . Je ne saurais parler.
ÉLIANTE. Que votre esprit un peu tâche à se rappeler.
ALCESTE. O juste Ciel ! faut-il qu'on joigne à tant de grâces 5
Les vices odieux des âmes les plus basses ?
ÉLIANTE. Mais encor qui vous peut. . . ?
ALCESTE. Ah ! tout est ruiné ;
Je suis, je suis trahi, je suis assassiné :
Célimène. . . . Eût-on pu croire cette nouvelle ? 10
Célimène me trompe, et n'est qu'une infidèle.
ÉLIANTE. Avez-vous pour le croire un juste fondement ?
PHILINTE. Peut-être est-ce un soupçon conçu légèrement,
Et votre esprit jaloux prend parfois des chimères. . . .
ALCESTE. Ah, morbleu ! mêlez-vous, monsieur, de vos affaires. 15
C'est de sa trahison n'être que trop certain,
Que l'avoir, dans ma poche, écrite de sa main.
Oui, madame, une lettre écrite pour Oronte
A produit à mes yeux ma disgrâce et sa honte ; 20
Oronte, dont j'ai cru qu'elle fuyait les soins,
Et que de mes rivaux je redoutais le moins.
PHILINTE. Une lettre peut bien tromper par l'apparence,
Et n'est pas quelquefois si coupable qu'on pense.
ALCESTE. Monsieur, encore un coup, laissez-moi, s'il vous plaît, 25
Et ne prenez souci que de votre intérêt.
ÉLIANTE. Vous devez modérer vos transports, et l'outrage. . .
ALCESTE. Madame, c'est à vous qu'appartient cet ouvrage ; 30
C'est à vous que mon cœur a recours aujourd'hui,
Pour pouvoir s'affranchir de son cuisant ennui.
Vengez-moi d'une ingrate et perfide parente,
Qui trahit lâchement une ardeur si constante ;
Vengez-moi de ce trait qui doit vous faire horreur. 35

ELIANTE. Moi, vous venger ! Comment ?
ALCESTE. En recevant mon cœur.
Acceptez-le, madame, au lieu de l'infidèle :
C'est par là que je puis prendre vengeance d'elle ; 5
Et je la veux punir par les sincères vœux,
Par le profond amour, les soins respectueux,
Les devoirs empressés et l'assidu service
Dont ce cœur va vous faire un ardent sacrifice.
ÉLIANTE. Je compatis, sans doute, à ce que vous souffrez, 10
Et ne méprise point le cœur que vous m'offrez ;
Mais peut-être le mal n'est pas si grand qu'on pense,
Et vous pourrez quitter ce désir de vengeance.
Lorsque l'injure part d'un objet plein d'appas,
On fait force desseins qu'on n'exécute pas : 15
On a beau voir, pour rompre, une raison puissante,
Une coupable aimée est bientôt innocente ;
Tout le mal qu'on lui veut se dissipe aisément,
Et l'on sait ce que c'est qu'un courroux d'un amant.
ALCESTE. Non, non, madame, non : l'offense est trop mortelle, 20
Il n'est point de retour, et je romps avec elle ;
Rien ne saurait changer le dessein que j'en fais,
Et je me punirais de l'estimer jamais.
La voici. Mon courroux redouble à cette approche ; 25
Je vais de sa noirceur lui faire un vif reproche,
Pleinement la confondre, et vous porter après
Un cœur tout dégagé de ses trompeurs attraits.

## SCÈNE III

*Célimène, Alceste*

ALCESTE. O ciel ! de mes transports puis-je être ici le maître ? 30

CÉLIMÈNE. Ouais ! Quel est donc le trouble où je vous vois paraître ?
Et que me veulent dire et ces soupirs poussés,
Et ces sombres regards que sur moi vous lancez ?
ALCESTE. Que toutes les horreurs dont une âme est capable 5
A vos déloyautés n'ont rien de comparable ;
Que le sort, les démons, et le Ciel en courroux
N'ont jamais rien produit de si méchant que vous.
CÉLIMÈNE. Voilà certainement des douceurs que j'admire.
ALCESTE. Ah ! ne plaisantez point, il n'est pas temps de rire : 10
Rougissez bien plutôt, vous en avez raison ;
Et j'ai de sûrs témoins de votre trahison.
Voilà ce que marquaient les troubles de mon âme ;
Ce n'était pas en vain que s'alarmait ma flamme ; 15
Par ces fréquents soupçons qu'on trouvait odieux,
Je cherchais le malheur qu'ont rencontré mes yeux ;
Et malgré tous vos soins et votre adresse à feindre,
Mon astre me disait ce que j'avais à craindre.
Mais ne présumez pas que, sans être vengé, 20
Je souffre le dépit de me voir outragé.
Je sais que sur les vœux on n'a point de puissance,
Que l'amour veut partout naître sans dépendance,
Que jamais par la force on n'entra dans un cœur,
Et que toute âme est libre à nommer son vainqueur. 25
Aussi ne trouverais-je aucun sujet de plainte,
Si pour moi votre bouche avait parlé sans feinte ;
Et, rejetant mes vœux dès le premier abord,
Mon cœur n'aurait eu droit de s'en prendre qu'au sort.
Mais d'un aveu trompeur voir ma flamme applaudie, 30
C'est une trahison, c'est une perfidie,
Qui ne saurait trouver de trop grands châtiments,
Et je puis tout permettre à mes ressentiments.
Oui, oui, redoutez tout après un tel outrage ;
Je ne suis plus à moi, je suis tout à la rage : 35

Percé du coup mortel dont vous m'assassinez,
Mes sens par la raison ne sont plus gouvernés,
Je cède aux mouvements d'une juste colère,
Et je ne réponds pas de ce que je puis faire.

CÉLIMÈNE. D'où vient donc, je vous prie, un tel emportement ? 5
Avez-vous, dites-moi, perdu le jugement ?

ALCESTE. Oui, oui, je l'ai perdu, lorsque dans votre vue
J'ai pris, pour mon malheur, le poison qui me tue,
Et que j'ai cru trouver quelque sincérité 10
Dans les traîtres appas dont je fus enchanté.

CÉLIMÈNE. De quelle trahison pouvez-vous donc vous plaindre ?

ALCESTE. Ah ! que ce cœur est double, et sait bien l'art de feindre ! 15
Mais, pour le mettre à bout, j'ai des moyens tout prêts :
Jetez ici les yeux, et connaissez vos traits :
Ce billet découvert suffit pour vous confondre,
Et contre ce témoin on n'a rien à répondre.

CÉLIMÈNE. Voilà donc le sujet qui vous trouble l'esprit ? 20

ALCESTE. Vous ne rougissez pas en voyant cet écrit ?

CÉLIMÈNE. Et par quelle raison faut-il que j'en rougisse ?

ALCESTE. Quoi ? vous joignez ici l'audace à l'artifice ?
Le désavouerez-vous, pour n'avoir point de seing ?

CÉLIMÈNE. Pourquoi désavouer un billet de ma main ? 25

ALCESTE. Et vous pouvez le voir sans demeurer confuse
Du crime dont vers moi son style vous accuse ?

CÉLIMÈNE. Vous êtes, sans mentir, un grand extravagant.

ALCESTE. Quoi ? vous bravez ainsi ce témoin convaincant ?
Et ce qu'il m'a fait voir de douceur pour Oronte 30
N'a donc rien qui m'outrage, et qui vous fasse honte ?

CÉLIMÈNE. Oronte ! Qui vous dit que la lettre est pour lui ?

ALCESTE. Les gens qui dans mes mains l'ont remise aujourd'hui. 35

Mais je veux consentir qu'elle soit pour un autre :
Mon cœur en a-t-il moins à se plaindre du vôtre ?
En serez-vous vers moi moins coupable en effet ?

CÉLIMÈNE. Mais si c'est une femme à qui va ce billet,
En quoi vous blesse-t-il ? et qu'a-t-il de coupable ? 5

ALCESTE. Ah ! le détour est bon, et l'excuse admirable.
Je ne m'attendais pas, je l'avoue, à ce trait,
Et me voilà, par là, convaincu tout à fait.
Osez-vous recourir à ces ruses grossières ?
Et croyez-vous les gens si privés de lumières ? 10
Voyons, voyons un peu par quel biais, de quel air,
Vous voulez soutenir un mensonge si clair,
Et comment vous pourrez tourner pour une femme
Tous les mots d'un billet qui montre tant de flamme ?
Ajustez, pour couvrir un manquement de foi, 15
Ce que je m'en vais lire. . . .

CÉLIMÈNE. Il ne me plaît pas, moi.
Je vous trouve plaisant d'user d'un tel empire,
Et de me dire au nez ce que vous m'osez dire.

ALCESTE. Non, non : sans s'emporter, prenez un peu souci 20
De me justifier les termes que voici.

CÉLIMÈNE. Non, je n'en veux rien faire ; et, dans cette occurrence,
Tout ce que vous croirez m'est de peu d'importance.

ALCESTE. De grâce, montrez-moi, je serai satisfait, 25
Qu'on peut pour une femme expliquer ce billet.

CÉLIMÈNE. Non, il est pour Oronte, et je veux qu'on le croie ;
Je reçois tous ses soins avec beaucoup de joie ;
J'admire ce qu'il dit, j'estime ce qu'il est, 30
Et je tombe d'accord de tout ce qu'il vous plaît.
Faites, prenez parti, que rien ne vous arrête,
Et ne me rompez pas davantage la tête.

ALCESTE. Ciel ! rien de plus cruel peut-il être inventé ?
Et jamais cœur fut-il de la sorte traité ? 35

Quoi ? d'un juste courroux je suis ému contre elle,
C'est moi qui me viens plaindre, et c'est moi qu'on
querelle !
On pousse ma douleur et mes soupçons à bout,
On me laisse tout croire, on fait gloire de tout ; 5
Et cependant mon cœur est encore assez lâche
Pour ne pouvoir briser la chaîne qui l'attache,
Et pour ne pas s'armer d'un généreux mépris
Contre l'ingrat objet dont il est trop épris !
Ah ! que vous savez bien ici, contre moi-même, 10
Perfide, vous servir de ma faiblesse extrême,
Et ménager pour vous l'excès prodigieux
De ce fatal amour né de vos traîtres yeux !
Défendez-vous au moins d'un crime qui m'accable,
Et cessez d'affecter d'être envers moi coupable ; 15
Rendez-moi, s'il se peut, ce billet innocent ;
A vous prêter les mains ma tendresse consent ;
Efforcez-vous ici de paraître fidèle,
Et je m'efforcerai, moi, de vous croire telle.

CÉLIMÈNE. Allez, vous êtes fou, dans vos transports jaloux, 20
Et ne méritez pas l'amour qu'on a pour vous.
Je voudrais bien savoir qui pourrait me contraindre
A descendre pour vous aux bassesses de feindre,
Et pourquoi, si mon cœur penchait d'autre côté,
Je ne le dirais pas avec sincérité. 25
Quoi ? de mes sentiments l'obligeante assurance
Contre tous vos soupçons ne prend pas ma défense ?
Auprès d'un tel garant, sont-ils de quelque poids ?
N'est-ce pas m'outrager que d'écouter leur voix ?
Et puisque notre cœur fait un effort extrême 30
Lorsqu'il peut se résoudre à confesser qu'il aime,
Puisque l'honneur du sexe, ennemi de nos feux,
S'oppose fortement à de pareils aveux,
L'amant qui voit pour lui franchir un tel obstacle
Doit-il impunément douter de cet oracle ? 35

Et n'est-il pas coupable en ne s'assurant pas
A ce qu'on ne dit point qu'après de grands combats ?
Allez, de tels soupçons méritent ma colère,
Et vous ne valez pas que l'on vous considère :
Je suis sotte, et veux mal à ma simplicité 5
De conserver encor pour vous quelque bonté ;
Je devrais autre part attacher mon estime,
Et vous faire un sujet de plainte légitime.

ALCESTE. Ah ! traîtresse, mon faible est étrange pour vous ; 10
Vous me trompez sans doute avec des mots si doux ;
Mais il n'importe, il faut suivre ma destinée ;
A votre foi mon âme est toute abandonnée ;
Je veux voir, jusqu'au bout, quel sera votre cœur,
Et si de me trahir il aura la noirceur. 15

CÉLIMÈNE. Non, vous ne m'aimez point comme il faut que l'on aime.

ALCESTE. Ah ! rien n'est comparable à mon amour extrême ;
Et dans l'ardeur qu'il a de se montrer à tous, 20
Il va jusqu'à former des souhaits contre vous.
Oui, je voudrais qu'aucun ne vous trouvât aimable,
Que vous fussiez réduite en un sort misérable,
Que le Ciel, en naissant, ne vous eût donné rien,
Que vous n'eussiez ni rang, ni naissance, ni bien, 25
Afin que de mon cœur l'éclatant sacrifice
Vous pût d'un pareil sort réparer l'injustice,
Et que j'eusse la joie et la gloire, en ce jour,
De vous voir tenir tout des mains de mon amour.

CÉLIMÈNE. C'est me vouloir du bien d'une étrange manière ! 30
Me préserve le Ciel que vous ayez matière. . . !
Voici monsieur Dubois plaisamment figuré.

## SCÈNE IV

*Dubois, Célimène, Alceste*

ALCESTE. Que veut cet équipage et cet air effaré ?
Qu'as-tu ?
DUBOIS. Monsieur. . . .
ALCESTE. Hé bien ?
DUBOIS. Voici bien des mystères. 5
ALCESTE. Qu'est-ce ?
DUBOIS. Nous sommes mal, monsieur, dans nos affaires.
ALCESTE. Quoi ?
DUBOIS. Parlerai-je haut ? 10
ALCESTE. Oui, parle, et promptement.
DUBOIS. N'est-il point là quelqu'un. . . ?
ALCESTE. Ah ! que d'amusement !
Veux-tu parler ?
DUBOIS. Monsieur, il faut faire retraite. 15
ALCESTE. Comment ?
DUBOIS. Il faut d'ici déloger sans trompette.
ALCESTE. Et pourquoi ?
DUBOIS. Je vous dis qu'il faut quitter ce lieu.
ALCESTE. La cause ? 20
DUBOIS. Il faut partir, monsieur, sans dire adieu.
ALCESTE. Mais par quelle raison me tiens-tu ce langage ?
DUBOIS. Par la raison, monsieur, qu'il faut plier bagage.
ALCESTE. Ah ! je te casserai la tête assurément,
Si tu ne veux, maraud, t'expliquer autrement. 25
DUBOIS. Monsieur, un homme noir et d'habit et de mine
Est venu nous laisser, jusque dans la cuisine,
Un papier griffonné d'une telle façon,
Qu'il faudrait, pour le lire, être pis qu'un démon.
C'est de votre procès, je n'en fais aucun doute ; 30
Mais le diable d'enfer, je crois, n'y verrait goutte.

ALCESTE. Hé bien ? quoi ? ce papier, qu'a-t-il à démêler,
Traître, avec le départ dont tu viens me parler ?
DUBOIS. C'est pour vous dire ici, monsieur, qu'une heure ensuite,
Un homme qui souvent vous vient rendre visite 5
Est venu vous chercher avec empressement,
Et, ne vous trouvant pas, m'a chargé doucement,
Sachant que je vous sers avec beaucoup de zèle,
De vous dire. . . . Attendez, comme est-ce qu'il s'appelle ? 10
ALCESTE. Laisse là son nom, traître, et dis ce qu'il t'a dit.
DUBOIS. C'est un de vos amis enfin, cela suffit.
Il m'a dit que d'ici votre péril vous chasse,
Et que d'être arrêté le sort vous y menace.
ALCESTE. Mais quoi ? n'a-t-il voulu te rien spécifier ? 15
DUBOIS. Non : il m'a demandé de l'encre et du papier,
Et vous a fait un mot, où vous pourrez, je pense,
Du fond de ce mystère avoir la connaissance.
ALCESTE. Donne-le donc.
CÉLIMÈNE. Que peut envelopper ceci ? 20
ALCESTE. Je ne sais ; mais j'aspire à m'en voir éclairci.
Auras-tu bientôt fait, impertinent au diable ?
DUBOIS, *après l'avoir longtemps cherché.* Ma foi, je l'ai, monsieur, laissé sur votre table.
ALCESTE. Je ne sais qui me tient. . . . 25
CÉLIMÈNE. Ne vous emportez pas,
Et courez démêler un pareil embarras.
ALCESTE. Il semble que le sort, quelque soin que je prenne,
Ait juré d'empêcher que je vous entretienne ;
Mais, pour en triompher, souffrez à mon amour 30
De vous revoir, madame, avant la fin du jour.

# ACTE V

## SCÈNE PREMIÈRE

*Alceste, Philinte*

ALCESTE. La résolution en est prise, vous dis-je.
PHILINTE. Mais, quel que soit ce coup, faut-il qu'il vous
   oblige . . . ?
ALCESTE. Non : vous avez beau faire et beau me raisonner,
   Rien de ce que je dis ne me peut détourner ; 5
   Trop de perversité règne au siècle où nous sommes,
   Et je veux me tirer du commerce des hommes.
   Quoi ? contre ma partie on voit tout à la fois
   L'honneur, la probité, la pudeur, et les lois ;
   On publie en tous lieux l'équité de ma cause ; 10
   Sur la foi de mon droit mon âme se repose :
   Cependant je me vois trompé par le succès ;
   J'ai pour moi la justice, et je perds mon procès !
   Un traître, dont on sait la scandaleuse histoire,
   Est sorti triomphant d'une fausseté noire ! 15
   Toute la bonne foi cède à sa trahison !
   Il trouve, en m'égorgeant, moyen d'avoir raison !
   Le poids de sa grimace, où brille l'artifice,
   Renverse le bon droit, et tourne la justice !
   Il fait par un arrêt couronner son forfait ! 20
   Et non content encor du tort que l'on me fait,
   Il court parmi le monde un livre abominable,
   Et de qui la lecture est même condamnable,
   Un livre à mériter la dernière rigueur,
   Dont le fourbe a le front de me faire l'auteur ! 25
   Et là-dessus on voit Oronte qui murmure,
   Et tâche méchamment d'appuyer l'imposture !
   Lui, qui d'un honnête homme à la cour tient le rang,

A qui je n'ai rien fait qu'être sincère et franc,
Qui me vient, malgré moi, d'une ardeur empressée,
Sur des vers qu'il a faits demander ma pensée ;
Et parce que j'en use avec honnêteté,
Et ne le veux trahir, lui ni la vérité, 5
Il aide à m'accabler d'un crime imaginaire !
Le voilà devenu mon plus grand adversaire !
Et jamais de son cœur je n'aurai de pardon,
Pour n'avoir pas trouvé que son sonnet fût bon !
Et les hommes, morbleu ! sont faits de cette sorte ! 10
C'est à ces actions que la gloire les porte !
Voilà la bonne foi, le zèle vertueux,
La justice et l'honneur que l'on trouve chez eux !
Allons, c'est trop souffrir les chagrins qu'on nous forge :
Tirons-nous de ce bois et de ce coupe-gorge. 15
Puisque entre humains ainsi vous vivez en vrais loups,
Traîtres ! vous ne m'aurez de ma vie avec vous.

PHILINTE. Je trouve un peu bien prompt le dessein où vous êtes,
Et tout le mal n'est pas si grand que vous le faites : 20
Ce que votre partie ose vous imputer
N'a point eu le crédit de vous faire arrêter ;
On voit son faux rapport lui-même se détruire,
Et c'est une action qui pourrait bien lui nuire.

ALCESTE. Lui ? De semblables tours il ne craint point l'éclat : 25
Il a permission d'être franc scélérat ;
Et loin qu'à son crédit nuise cette aventure,
On l'en verra demain en meilleure posture.

PHILINTE. Enfin il est constant qu'on n'a point trop donné 30
Au bruit que contre vous sa malice a tourné ;
De ce côté déjà vous n'avez rien à craindre :
Et pour votre procès, dont vous pouvez vous plaindre,
Il vous est en justice aisé d'y revenir,
Et contre cet arrêt. . . 35

ALCESTE. Non : je veux m'y tenir.
Quelque sensible tort qu'un tel arrêt me fasse,
Je me garderai bien de vouloir qu'on le casse :
On y voit trop à plein le bon droit maltraité,
Et je veux qu'il demeure à la postérité 5
Comme une marque insigne, un fameux témoignage
De la méchanceté des hommes de notre âge.
Ce sont vingt mille francs qu'il m'en pourra coûter ;
Mais, pour vingt mille francs, j'aurai droit de pester
Contre l'iniquité de la nature humaine, 10
Et de nourrir pour elle une immortelle haine.

PHILINTE. Mais enfin. . . .

ALCESTE. Mais enfin, vos soins sont superflus :
Que pouvez-vous, monsieur, me dire là-dessus ? 15
Aurez-vous bien le front de me vouloir, en face,
Excuser les horreurs de tout ce qui se passe ?

PHILINTE. Non : je tombe d'accord de tout ce qu'il vous plaît :
Tout marche par cabale et par pur intérêt ; 20
Ce n'est plus que la ruse aujourd'hui qui l'emporte,
Et les hommes devraient être faits d'autre sorte.
Mais est-ce une raison que leur peu d'équité
Pour vouloir se tirer de leur société ?
Tous ces défauts humains nous donnent, dans la vie, 25
Des moyens d'exercer notre philosophie :
C'est le plus bel emploi que trouve la vertu ;
Et si de probité tout était revêtu,
Si tous les cœurs étaient francs, justes et dociles,
La plupart des vertus nous seraient inutiles, 30
Puisqu'on en met l'usage à pouvoir sans ennui
Supporter, dans nos droits, l'injustice d'autrui ;
Et de même qu'un cœur d'une vertu profonde. . . .

ALCESTE. Je sais que vous parlez, monsieur, le mieux du monde : 35

En beaux raisonnements vous abondez toujours ;
Mais vous perdez le temps et tous vos beaux discours.
La raison, pour mon bien, veut que je me retire :
Je n'ai point sur ma langue un assez grand empire ;
De ce que je dirais je ne répondrais pas, 5
Et je me jetterais cent choses sur les bras.
Laissez-moi, sans dispute, attendre Célimène :
Il faut qu'elle consente au dessein qui m'amène :
Je vais voir si son cœur a de l'amour pour moi,
Et c'est ce moment-ci qui doit m'en faire foi. 10

PHILINTE. Montons chez Éliante, attendant sa venue.

ALCESTE. Non : de trop de souci je me sens l'âme émue.
Allez-vous-en la voir, et me laissez enfin
Dans ce petit coin sombre, avec mon noir chagrin.

PHILINTE. C'est une compagnie étrange pour attendre, 15
Et je vais obliger Éliante à descendre.

## SCÈNE II

*Oronte, Célimène, Alceste*

ORONTE. Oui, c'est à vous de voir si par des nœuds si doux,
Madame, vous voulez m'attacher tout à vous.
Il me faut de votre âme une pleine assurance :
Un amant là-dessus n'aime point qu'on balance. 20
Si l'ardeur de mes feux a pu vous émouvoir,
Vous ne devez point feindre à me le faire voir ;
Et la preuve, après tout, que je vous en demande,
C'est de ne plus souffrir qu'Alceste vous prétende,
De le sacrifier, madame, à mon amour, 25
Et de chez vous enfin le bannir dès ce jour.

CÉLIMÈNE. Mais quel sujet si grand contre lui vous irrite,
Vous à qui j'ai tant vu parler de son mérite ?

ORONTE. Madame, il ne faut point ces éclaircissements ;
Il s'agit de savoir quels sont vos sentiments. 30

ALCESTE.

*Oui, monsieur a raison; madame, il faut choisir;*
*Et sa demande ici s'accorde à mon desir.*

Le Misanthrope, Acte V. Sc 2.

Choisissez, s'il vous plaît, de garder l'un ou l'autre ;
Ma résolution n'attend rien que la vôtre.

ALCESTE, *sortant du coin où il s'était retiré*. Oui, monsieur a raison : madame, il faut choisir,
Et sa demande ici s'accorde à mon désir. 5
Pareille ardeur me presse, et même soin m'amène ;
Mon amour veut du vôtre une marque certaine,
Les choses ne sont plus pour traîner en longueur,
Et voici le moment d'expliquer votre cœur.

ORONTE. Je ne veux point, monsieur, d'une flamme importune 10
Troubler aucunement votre bonne fortune.

ALCESTE. Je ne veux point, monsieur, jaloux ou non jaloux,
Partager de son cœur rien du tout avec vous.

ORONTE. Si votre amour au mien lui semble préférable.... 15

ALCESTE. Si du moindre penchant elle est pour vous capable....

ORONTE. Je jure de n'y rien prétendre désormais.

ALCESTE. Je jure hautement de ne la voir jamais.

ORONTE. Madame, c'est à vous de parler sans contrainte. 20

ALCESTE. Madame, vous pouvez vous expliquer sans crainte.

ORONTE. Vous n'avez qu'à nous dire où s'attachent vos vœux.

ALCESTE. Vous n'avez qu'à trancher, et choisir de nous deux. 25

ORONTE. Quoi ? sur un pareil choix vous semblez être en peine !

ALCESTE. Quoi ? votre âme balance, et paraît incertaine !

CÉLIMÈNE. Mon Dieu ! que cette instance est là hors de saison, 30
Et que vous témoignez, tous deux, peu de raison !
Je sais prendre parti sur cette préférence,
Et ce n'est pas mon cœur maintenant qui balance :
Il n'est point suspendu, sans doute, entre vous deux, 35

Et rien n'est si tôt fait que le choix de nos vœux.
Mais je souffre, à vrai dire, une gêne trop forte
A prononcer en face un aveu de la sorte :
Je trouve que ces mots, qui sont désobligeants,
Ne se doivent point dire en présence des gens ; 5
Qu'un cœur de son penchant donne assez de lumière,
Sans qu'on nous fasse aller jusqu'à rompre en visière ;
Et qu'il suffit enfin que de plus doux témoins
Instruisent un amant du malheur de ses soins.

ORONTE. Non, non, un franc aveu n'a rien que j'appréhende ; 10
J'y consens pour ma part.

ALCESTE. Et moi, je le demande ;
C'est son éclat surtout qu'ici j'ose exiger,
Et je ne prétends point vous voir rien ménager. 15
Conserver tout le monde est votre grande étude :
Mais plus d'amusement, et plus d'incertitude ;
Il faut vous expliquer nettement là-dessus,
Ou bien pour un arrêt je prends votre refus ;
Je saurai, de ma part, expliquer ce silence, 20
Et me tiendrai pour dit tout le mal que j'en pense.

ORONTE. Je vous sais fort bon gré, monsieur, de ce courroux,
Et je lui dis ici même chose que vous.

CÉLIMÈNE. Que vous me fatiguez avec un tel caprice !
Ce que vous demandez a-t-il de la justice ? 25
Et ne vous dis-je pas quel motif me retient ?
J'en vais prendre pour juge Éliante qui vient.

## SCÈNE III

*Éliante, Philinte, Célimène, Oronte, Alceste*

CÉLIMÈNE. Je me vois, ma cousine, ici persécutée
Par des gens dont l'humeur y paraît concertée.
Ils veulent, l'un et l'autre, avec même chaleur, 30

Que je prononce entre eux le choix que fait mon cœur,
Et que, par un arrêt qu'en face il me faut rendre,
Je défende à l'un d'eux tous les soins qu'il peut prendre.
Dites-moi si jamais cela se fait ainsi.
ÉLIANTE. N'allez point là-dessus me consulter ici ; 5
Peut-être y pourriez-vous être mal adressée,
Et je suis pour les gens qui disent leur pensée.
ORONTE. Madame, c'est en vain que vous vous défendez.
ALCESTE. Tous vos détours ici seront mal secondés.
ORONTE. Il faut, il faut parler, et lâcher la balance. 10
ALCESTE. Il ne faut que poursuivre à garder le silence.
ORONTE. Je ne veux qu'un seul mot pour finir nos débats.
ALCESTE. Et moi, je vous entends si vous ne parlez pas.

## SCÈNE DERNIÈRE

*Acaste, Clitandre, Arsinoé, Philinte, Éliante, Oronte, Célimène, Alceste*

ACASTE. Madame, nous venons tous deux, sans vous déplaire, 15
Éclaircir avec vous une petite affaire.
CLITANDRE. Fort à propos, messieurs, vous vous trouvez ici,
Et vous êtes mêlés dans cette affaire aussi.
ARSINOÉ. Madame, vous serez surprise de ma vue ; 20
Mais ce sont ces messieurs qui causent ma venue :
Tous deux ils m'ont trouvée, et se sont plaints à moi
D'un trait à qui mon cœur ne saurait prêter foi.
J'ai du fond de votre âme une trop haute estime,
Pour vous croire jamais capable d'un tel crime ; 25
Mes yeux ont démenti leurs témoins les plus forts ;
Et l'amitié passant sur de petits discords,
J'ai bien voulu chez vous leur faire compagnie,
Pour vous voir vous laver de cette calomnie.

ACASTE. Oui, madame, voyons, d'un esprit adouci,
Comment vous vous prendrez à soutenir ceci.
Cette lettre par vous est écrite à Clitandre ?
CLITANDRE. Vous avez pour Acaste écrit ce billet tendre ?
ACASTE. Messieurs, ces traits pour vous n'ont point d'obscurité, 5
Et je ne doute pas que sa civilité
A connaître sa main n'ait trop su vous instruire
Mais ceci vaut assez la peine de le lire :
*Vous êtes un étrange homme de condamner mon enjouement, et de me reprocher que je n'ai jamais tant de joie que lorsque je ne suis pas avec vous. Il n'y a rien de plus injuste ; et si vous ne venez bien vite me demander pardon de cette offense, je ne vous la pardonnerai de ma vie. Notre grand flandrin de vicomte. . . .* 10
Il devrait être ici. 15
*Notre grand flandrin de vicomte, par qui vous commencez vos plaintes, est un homme qui ne saurait me revenir ; et depuis que je l'ai vu, trois quarts d'heure durant, cracher dans un puits pour faire des ronds, je n'ai pu jamais prendre bonne opinion de lui. Pour le petit marquis. . . .* 20
C'est moi-même, messieurs, sans nulle vanité.
*Pour le petit marquis, qui me tint hier longtemps la main, je trouve qu'il n'y a rien de si mince que toute sa personne ; et ce sont de ces mérites qui n'ont que la cape et l'épée. Pour l'homme aux rubans verts. . . .* 25
A vous le dé, monsieur.
*Pour l'homme aux rubans verts, il me divertit quelquefois avec ses brusqueries et son chagrin bourru; mais il est cent moments où je le trouve le plus fâcheux du monde. Et pour l'homme à la veste. . . .*
Voici votre paquet. 30
*Et pour l'homme à la veste, qui s'est jeté dans le bel esprit et veut être auteur malgré tout le monde, je ne puis me donner la peine d'écouter ce qu'il dit ; et sa prose me fatigue autant que ses vers. Mettez-vous donc en tête que je ne me divertis pas toujours si bien que vous pensez ; que je vous trouve à dire plus* 35

*que je ne voudrais, dans toutes les parties où l'on m'entraîne ; et que c'est un merveilleux assaisonnement aux plaisirs qu'on goûte que la présence des gens qu'on aime.*

CLITANDRE. Me voici maintenant, moi.

*Votre Clitandre dont vous me parlez, et qui fait tant le doucereux, est le dernier des hommes pour qui j'aurais de l'amitié. Il est extravagant de se persuader qu'on l'aime ; et vous l'êtes de croire qu'on ne vous aime pas. Changez, pour être raisonnable, vos sentiments contre les siens ; et voyez-moi le plus que vous pourrez, pour m'aider à porter le chagrin d'en être obsédée.* 10

D'un fort beau caractère on voit là le modèle,
Madame, et vous savez comment cela s'appelle ?
Il suffit : nous allons, l'un et l'autre, en tous lieux
Montrer de votre cœur le portrait glorieux.

ACASTE. J'aurais de quoi vous dire, et belle est la matière ; 15
Mais je ne vous tiens pas digne de ma colère ;
Et je vous ferai voir que les petits marquis
Ont, pour se consoler, des cœurs du plus haut prix.

ORONTE. Quoi ? de cette façon je vois qu'on me déchire,
Après tout ce qu'à moi je vous ai vu m'écrire ! 20
Et votre cœur, paré de beaux semblants d'amour,
A tout le genre humain se promet tour à tour !
Allez, j'étais trop dupe, et je vais ne plus l'être ;
Vous me faites un bien, me faisant vous connaître :
J'y profite d'un cœur qu'ainsi vous me rendez, 25
Et trouve ma vengeance en ce que vous perdez.

*A Alceste.*

Monsieur, je ne fais plus d'obstacle à votre flamme,
Et vous pouvez conclure affaire avec madame.

ARSINOÉ. Certes, voilà le trait du monde le plus noir ; 30
Je ne m'en saurais taire, et me sens émouvoir.
Voit-on des procédés qui soient pareils aux vôtres ?
Je ne prends point de part aux intérêts des autres ;
Mais monsieur, que chez vous fixait votre bonheur,
Un homme, comme lui, de mérite et d'honneur, 35

Et qui vous chérissait avec idolâtrie,
Devait-il. . . ?

ALCESTE. Laissez-moi, madame, je vous prie,
Vider mes intérêts moi-même là-dessus,
Et ne vous chargez point de ces soins superflus. 5
Mon cœur a beau vous voir prendre ici sa querelle,
Il n'est point en état de payer ce grand zèle ;
Et ce n'est pas à vous que je pourrai songer,
Si par un autre choix je cherche à me venger.

ARSINOÉ. Hé! croyez-vous, monsieur, qu'on ait cette pensée, 10
Et que de vous avoir on soit tant empressée ?
Je vous trouve un esprit bien plein de vanité,
Si de cette créance il peut s'être flatté.
Le rebut de madame est une marchandise
Dont on aurait grand tort d'être si fort éprise. 15
Détrompez-vous, de grâce, et portez-le moins haut :
Ce ne sont pas des gens comme moi qu'il vous faut ;
Vous ferez bien encor de soupirer pour elle,
Et je brûle de voir une union si belle. [*Elle se retire.*]

ALCESTE. Hé bien ! je me suis tu, malgré ce que je voi, 20
Et j'ai laissé parler tout le monde avant moi :
Ai-je pris sur moi-même un assez long empire,
Et puis-je maintenant. . . ?

CÉLIMÈNE. Oui, vous pouvez tout dire ;
Vous en êtes en droit, lorsque vous vous plaindrez, 25
Et de me reprocher tout ce que vous voudrez.
J'ai tort, je le confesse, et mon âme confuse
Ne cherche à vous payer d'aucune vaine excuse.
J'ai des autres ici méprisé le courroux,
Mais je tombe d'accord de mon crime envers vous. 30
Votre ressentiment, sans doute, est raisonnable :
Je sais combien je dois vous paraître coupable,
Que toute chose dit que j'ai pu vous trahir,
Et qu'enfin vous avez sujet de me haïr.
Faites-le, j'y consens. 35

ALCESTE. Hé ! le puis-je, traîtresse ?
Puis-je ainsi triompher de toute ma tendresse ?
Et quoique avec ardeur je veuille vous haïr,
Trouvé-je un cœur en moi tout prêt à m'obéir ?
*A Éliante et Philinte.* 5
Vous voyez ce que peut une indigne tendresse,
Et je vous fais tous deux témoins de ma faiblesse.
Mais, à vous dire vrai, ce n'est pas encor tout,
Et vous allez me voir la pousser jusqu'au bout,
Montrer que c'est à tort que sages on nous nomme, 10
Et que dans tous les cœurs il est toujours de l'homme.
Oui, je veux bien, perfide, oublier vos forfaits ;
J'en saurai, dans mon âme, excuser tous les traits,
Et me les couvrirai du nom d'une faiblesse
Où le vice du temps porte votre jeunesse, 15
Pourvu que votre cœur veuille donner les mains
Au dessein que j'ai fait de fuir tous les humains,
Et que dans mon désert, où j'ai fait vœu de vivre,
Vous soyez, sans tarder, résolue à me suivre :
C'est par là seulement que, dans tous les esprits, 20
Vous pouvez réparer le mal de vos écrits,
Et qu'après cet éclat, qu'un noble cœur abhorre,
Il peut m'être permis de vous aimer encore.
CÉLIMÈNE. Moi, renoncer au monde avant que de vieillir,
Et dans votre désert aller m'ensevelir ! 25
ALCESTE. Et s'il faut qu'à mes feux votre flamme réponde,
Que vous doit importer tout le reste du monde ?
Vos désirs avec moi ne sont-ils pas contents ?
CÉLIMÈNE. La solitude effraye une âme de vingt ans ; 30
Je ne sens point la mienne assez grande, assez forte,
Pour me résoudre à prendre un dessein de la sorte.
Si le don de ma main peut contenter vos vœux,
Je pourrai me résoudre à serrer de tels nœuds ;
Et l'hymen. . . . 35

ALCESTE. Non : mon cœur à présent vous déteste,
Et ce refus lui seul fait plus que tout le reste.
Puisque vous n'êtes point, en des liens si doux,
Pour trouver tout en moi, comme moi tout en vous,
Allez, je vous refuse, et ce sensible outrage 5
De vos indignes fers pour jamais me dégage.

[*Célimène se retire, et Alceste parle à Éliante.*]

Madame, cent vertus ornent votre beauté,
Et je n'ai vu qu'en vous de la sincérité ;
De vous, depuis longtemps, je fais un cas extrême ; 10
Mais laissez-moi toujours vous estimer de même ;
Et souffrez que mon cœur, dans ses troubles divers,
Ne se présente point à l'honneur de vos fers :
Je m'en sens trop indigne, et commence à connaître
Que le Ciel pour ce nœud ne m'avait point fait naître ; 15
Que ce serait pour vous un hommage trop bas
Que le rebut d'un cœur qui ne vous valait pas ;
Et qu'enfin. . . .

ÉLIANTE. Vous pouvez suivre cette pensée :
Ma main de se donner n'est pas embarrassée, 20
Et voilà votre ami, sans trop m'inquiéter,
Qui, si je l'en priais, la pourrait accepter.

PHILINTE. Ah ! cet honneur, madame, est toute mon envie,
Et j'y sacrifierais et mon sang et ma vie. 25

ALCESTE. Puissiez-vous, pour goûter de vrais contentements,
L'un pour l'autre à jamais garder ces sentiments!
Trahi de toutes parts, accablé d'injustices,
Je vais sortir d'un gouffre où triomphent les vices, 30
Et chercher sur la terre un endroit écarté
Où d'être homme d'honneur on ait la liberté.

PHILINTE. Allons, madame, allons employer toute chose,
Pour rompre le dessein que son cœur se propose.

# NOTES

*(The figures refer to the page and line.)*

## ACT I

### SCENE I

**2.** 4. **bizarrerie:** ' caprice.'

5. **laissez-moi là:** ' leave me alone.'

11. **chagrins:** 'fits of anger or bad temper.' To-day *chagrin* is occasionally used in this sense, but its usual meaning is 'grief.'

13. **quoique amis:** although the meaning is clear, this elliptical construction is not quite correct grammatically, as the subjects of the two clauses are not the same.

14. **rayez . . . papiers:** ' don't count on that.' " On dit, *ôtez, rayez cela de dessus vos papiers,* pour dire : ne faites point votre compte là-dessus " (Dictionnaire de l'Académie, 1694).

16. **voir paraître:** ' to discover.'

17. **je vous déclare net:** ' I tell you point-blank ' ; ***net*** is an adjective used as an adverb.

19. **à votre compte:** ***à votre avis.***

21. **allez:** ' come now ! '

23. **s'en doit scandaliser:** in modern French, ***s'en*** would normally follow *doit,* for, when a verb is followed by a dependent infinitive, pronouns governed by the infinitive are usually placed immediately before it. The given construction could still be used in elevated speech. Molière uses this word-order very frequently throughout the play. Translate ' must be appalled by it.'

27. **fureur:** ' transports.' The sense of *charger de* with this noun is ' to lend greater vehemence to ' (literally ' to overload with ').

**4.** 1. **quel:** *qui.* This use was common in seventeenth-century French and is still possible to-day.

**4.** 2. comme: modern French would require *comment*; *comme* is nowadays primarily an adverb of degree, not of manner.

3. en vous séparant: 'when you part.' The participle is misrelated, as, grammatically, it goes with *chaleur*. The construction is permissible, however, as the meaning is sufficiently clear.

4. traitez: here *traiter* followed by *de* has the sense of 'to refer to as.'

5. morbleu: ''sdeath'; a corruption of (*par la*) *mort Dieu*. *Dieu* has the sense of a genitive; cf *Hôtel-Dieu*.

11. avoir pour agréable: 'to allow, agree to it.'

12. que . . . grâce: 'that I should grant myself pardon.'

22. monnoie: see Introduction, p. liv.

26. gens à la mode: 'people of fashion.'

29. embrassades: there is a note of contempt here, lacking in *embrassements* (p. 2, l. 27).

31. font combat: 'vie.'

32. honnête homme: 'gentleman, well-bred man.'

**5** 2. il n'est point d'âme: 'there is not a soul.' *Il est* for *il y a* is used only in lofty style in modern French. Molière uses it frequently throughout the play.

bien située: this rather unusual epithet probably means 'lofty' or 'noble.'

3. veuille de: 'would like.'

4. la plus glorieuse: this phrase seems to go more logically with *estime* than with *âme*, though both renderings are possible. The whole line is obscure.

7. qu'estimer: this would be *que d'estimer* in modern French.

8. y: the pronoun is redundant as it anticipates the following adverbial phrase, but it is used here for added emphasis.

9. vous . . . gens: 'you are not fit to be one of my friends.'

25. n'en déplaise à: 'with all due deference to'—the subjunctive is optative. This construction still survives in expressions such as *à Dieu ne plaise* ('God forbid').

28. mille gens: normally *gens* is not accompanied by a

numeral unless it is also qualified by an adjective; but *mille gens* is a stock phrase used to designate a large number of persons.

33. il sied mal . . . jolie: 'it ill becomes her to pose as a beauty.'

34. blanc: white cosmetic.

6. 3. à conter: 'by telling of.'

10. m'échauffer la bile: 'arouse my ire.'

17. rompre en visière à: a jousting term used metaphorically here to mean 'to quarrel openly with.'

18. philosophe: nowadays *philosophique* would be used, though *philosophe* is still used adjectivally with reference to persons.

19. où: in the seventeenth century, *où* was more often used than to-day in place of *dans* or *à* + relative pronoun.

20. mêmes: in modern French we would expect the definite article to precede *mêmes* as used here.

21. ces deux frères: an allusion to Ariste and Sganarelle in *l'École des maris*. Molière contrasts them in much the same way as he does Philinte and Alceste.

24. tout de bon: 'seriously, quite frankly.'

28. donne la comédie: 'gives rise to amusement.'

30. vous tourne en ridicule: 'makes you look ridiculous.' In Molière's day, *ridicule* could be used as an abstract noun = 'ridicule, ridiculousness,' or to denote a ridiculous person. There is, therefore, some ambiguity about this phrase, but certain critics are convinced that Molière intended the noun to refer to the person here. Nowadays, *ridicule* is not so used.

7. 4. seront: 'are to be.'

5. encore en est-il bien: 'at the same time there are many.'

9. pour être: *parce qu'ils sont.*

aux méchants complaisants: in modern French, *complaisant* takes *pour* or *envers.*

n'avoir pas: to-day we would prefer *ne pas avoir*, which is the normal modern usage when negation accompanies an infinitive.

franc: 'arrant.'

à plein: 'completely.'

7\. 18. **pied plat:** a term of contempt. "Dans son acception propre, il désignait l'homme sans naissance, le simple bourgeois qui portait des souliers plats, pendant que le gentilhomme avait des chaussures à hauts talons" (Lavigne). Translate 'contemptible fellow, wretch.'

25\. **n'y contredit:** this construction should be noted, since *contredire* used with a noun takes no preposition.

26\. **sa grimace:** 'his hypocrisy.'

29\. **honnête homme:** cf. note to page 4, line 32; the adjective may, of course, be used literally to mean 'honest.'

30\. **têtebleu:** 'zounds'; a corruption of *tête Dieu*. Cf. note to page 4, line 5.

31\. **avec . . . mesures:** 'any moderation is preserved in dealing with vice.'

8\. 10. **elle veut aux mortels:** 'it demands of mortals.'

16\. **voir paraître:** cf. note to page 2, line 16.

21\. **philosophe:** cf. note to page 6, line 18.

22\. **qui raisonne:** the 1682 edition gives *raisonnez*, which one would write nowadays. In the seventeenth century, however, the verb in a relative clause was often put in the third person, even when the antecedent was in the first or second person.

24\. **s'il faut:** 'should it happen.' Molière frequently uses this construction to stress possibility rather than necessity.

26\. **tâche à:** modern French would prefer *tâche de*.

9\. 3. **impertinence:** 'irrelevance.'

5\. **votre partie:** 'your adversary.'

8\. **qui pour vous sollicite:** 'to solicit the judges for you.' It was customary in Molière's day for the two parties engaged in a lawsuit to visit the judges in order to win their favour and protection.

18\. **en:** 'in the affair.'

27\. **succès:** 'issue, outcome.'

32\. **plaiderie:** 'lawsuit'—*procès* in modern French. Even in Molière's day, *plaiderie* was rarely used in this sense.

10\. 2. **m'en coûtât-il:** 'even though it should cost me.' The *en* has the sense of 'concerning it.' This subjunctive construction is still used to-day; cf. *écrivez-moi, ne fût-ce que quelques lignes*.

**10.** 3. grand'chose: the apostrophe does not denote here and in other similar expressions that there is elision of *e*, but that no feminine ending has been added to the stem. In medieval French, adjectives derived from Latin adjectives with only one form for masculine and feminine (e.g., *grandis*) show only one form for both genders in French; *grand'chose*, *grand'-mère*, etc., are relics of this peculiarity.

4. la beauté du fait: 'the beauty of it.'

5. tout de bon: cf. note to page 6, line 24.

6. de la façon: *de cette façon-là*. The definite article is here etymologically connected with Latin *illam*.

10. où: modern French would require *dans laquelle*. Cf. note to page 6, line 19.

11. ici: *i.e.*, Célimène's house.

15. chez lui: *i.e.*, *chez le genre humain*. Translate 'from its numbers.'

17. où: cf. note to page 6, line 19.

20. leurs vœux: 'their ardent desires.'

21. amuse: used here in the sense of 'beguiles.'

24. d'où vient que: 'how comes it about that.' To-day we would expect *il* after the verb.

25. ce qu'en . . . belle: 'the share of them which this damsel possesses.'

30. on lui treuve: 'are found in her'; *treuve* is an archaic form of *trouve* and even in Molière's own day it was not generally considered desirable. The court, which set the tone in such matters, used *trouve*.

**11.** 1. en dépit qu'on en ait: 'in spite of myself, against my better judgment.'

2. ma flamme: 'my passion.'

10. bien atteint: 'completely won over.'

16. solide: 'steadfast, dependable.'

17. conforme: 'appropriate'; in modern French *conforme* is usually followed by *à* and a noun.

était: used here as a conditional; cf. similar English use of 'were' in the translation 'were (*i.e.*, would be) more suitable.'

20. vos feux: 'your passion.'

## SCENE II

11\. 23. **su**: here equivalent to *appris*.
**là-bas**: 'downstairs.' Nowadays we should say *en bas*.
27\. **j'ai monté**: in modern French the auxiliary *être* would normally be expected with *monter* used absolutely.
29\. **m'a mis . . . désir**: the use of *mettre dans* with *désir* is unusual. Modern French would prefer *inspirer*.

12\. 16. **prétendre**: 'claim.' The transitive use of this verb was common in the seventeenth century, but is now less frequent.
22\. **de ma part**: 'for my part'; *pour ma part* in modern French.
26\. **sois-je**: 'may I be.'
**du ciel**: *par le ciel* in modern French.

13\. 1. **mystère**: 'reserve.'
3\. **mettre**: *employer*.
4\. **avec lumière . . . naître**: 'such a union must be born of judgment and discrimination.'
5\. **avant que nous lier**: modern French would require *avant que de nous lier* or, more commonly still, *avant de nous lier*.
6\. **telles complexions**: 'such dispositions, temperaments.' To-day *telles* would be preceded by *de*.
14\. **il en use**: 'he acts, deals.'
17\. **de grandes lumières**: 'great enlightenment, intelligence.'
26\. **j'aurais lieu de**: nowadays an infinitive, rather than a noun, follows this expression.
27\. **m'exposant**: cf. note to page 4, line 3.
**pour me parler**: *pour que vous me parliez*. Although the infinitive is misrelated, the construction is permissible since the meaning is clear.
29\. **puisque . . . ainsi**: 'since you would have it thus.' The verb *plaire* was used impersonally with a meaning equivalent to *vouloir*; cf. page 54, line 17.

14\. 9. **vous saurez que**: 'I would have you know that.'
16\. **marche après**: 'comes after.'
18\. The stage direction *bas* is given in the 1682 edition.

14. 30. trépas: 'death'—used chiefly in poetry and elevated style.
34. la chute: 'the conclusion, concluding idea.'

15. 1. empoisonneur au diable: 'the devil take you, you pest.' The dative here has a possessive sense. Some editors suggest that the phrase is elliptical for *digne d'aller au diable*.
3. en . . . une: 'if only you had made one'; *une*, which refers to *chute* in line 34, page 14, is here used with its literal meaning, 'a fall.' It is difficult to convey the pun satisfactorily in English.
15. bel esprit: 'wit.' It may also be used for a person of wit.
17. de sa façon: 'which he had composed.'
18. galant homme: 'well-bred man.'
empire: control.'
19. les démangeaisons: literally, *démangeaison* means 'itch,' and by extension, as here, 'the urge.'
21. faire éclat: 'display.'
23. de mauvais personnages: 'ludicrous rôles.'
28. à: nowadays *pour* would be used to express purpose.
29. qu'eût-on, d'autre part: 'though in other respects they may possess.'
32. pour ne point écrire: cf. note to page 13, line 27.
33. je lui mettais aux yeux: 'I brought to his notice. Modern French would prefer *sous les yeux*.
34. honnêtes: 'worthy.'

16. 3. qui: =*qu'est-ce qui*—a very rare use in modern French.
4. l'essor: 'publication.' The use of *essor* in this sense is unusual.
8. de quoi . . . somme: 'no matter by what means you are urged.'
15. bon à mettre au cabinet: 'fit to be relegated to a desk.'
25. sort du: 'is not in keeping with.'
29. tout grossiers: understood *qu'ils étaient*: 'unpolished as they were.'
31. je m'en vais vous dire: for *je vais vous dire*. This usage was common in the seventeenth century; it often implies 'to be about to.'

17. 3. au gué: a burden in folk-songs and popular poetry,

used generally to express joy; *oh gay!* in the 1734 edition.

7. dont . . . murmure: 'at which good sense complains, cries out.' The use here of *murmurer de* is uncommon.

19. beaux esprits: 'witty people.' Cf. note to page 15, line 15.

21. ces faux brillants: 'these false gems.' Referring to style, Littré defines *faux brillants* as follows: "pensées qui ont de l'éclat, mais un éclat trompeur, et s'évanouissant devant la moindre lumière."

33. je . . . approuviez: 'I can quite well do without your approval of them.'

18. 9. chez moi: 'with me.' Cf. *chez Molière.*

qui vous encense: 'someone to flatter you.'

11. prenez . . . haut: *le prendre haut* is elliptical for *le prendre sur le haut ton.* Translate 'speak in a rather less high and mighty fashion.'

17. This and the following lines are meant to be taken ironically.

## SCENE III

22. vous . . . affaire: 'there you are with an unpleasant affair on your hands.'

30. point de langage: 'no more words' (of explanation)

19. 5. on outrage: 'you insult me.'

# ACT II

## SCENE I

20. 2. mal satisfait: 'far from pleased'; preferably *mécontent* in modern French.

7. je vous promettrais . . . serais pas: 'even if I were to promise you the contrary . . . I should not be.'

11. humeur: 'disposition.'

14. amants: 'suitors, admirers.' To-day some other term such as *amoureux* would be used, as *amant* is not now used in this sense.

18. aimable: equivalent here to *digne d'être aimé.*

**20. 23. à leurs vœux moins facile:** 'less accessible to their protestations of love'; *facile à* is now rare.

**26. qui vous rend les armes:** 'whoever surrenders to you.'

**22. 6. l'heur:** 'the good fortune'—hardly ever used now except proverbially and in the compounds *bonheur*, *malheur*, etc.

**13. canons:** ornamental frills worn round the knees at the lower part of the *culotte*. They were decorated with ribbons, and, in Molière's time, it was fashionable in high circles to have them of excessive width. See illustration on page 63.

**15. rhingrave:** 'petticoat-breeches'—"culotte ou haut-de-chausse fort ample, attachée aux bas avec plusieurs rubans, dont un rhingrave . . . a amené la mode en France" (Furetière).

**16. faisant:** 'playing the part of'; cf. *faire l'innocent*.

**17. ton de fausset:** 'falsetto voice.'

**22. dans:** to-day *à* would be necessary here in the sense of 'to interest someone in something.' Nowadays *intéresser dans* = 'to give a financial interest in.'

**31. ramasser:** 'concentrate.'

**23. 5. la fleurette:** 'compliment.'

**16. à rompre:** *pour rompre*.

**24. en:** 'of it,' *i.e.*, 'of your love.'

**28. il ne tient qu'à vous . . . ne passe:** 'it depends on you alone . . .' The pleonastic *ne* is required in negative and interrogative clauses dependent on *il tient à*, but with *ne . . . que* this rule is variable.

**30. coupons chemin à:** 'let us put an end to.'

**31. voyons d'arrêter:** in modern French, *à* would be used instead of *de*. Molière uses both constructions, but here *de* is required for reasons of scansion and euphony. Translate 'let us contrive to stop.'

## SCENE II

**24. 2. là-bas:** cf. note to page 11, line 23.

**8. de tous:** modern French would require *entre* or *d'entre tous*. For rhyme *tous*, *vous*, cf. Introduction, page liii.

**10. je me fasse une affaire:** 'I should have a quarrel.'

24\. 12. **vous avez des regards**: 'you show consideration.' The 1682 edition substitutes *égards*, which suggests that *regards* used in this sense was not popular towards the end of the century. The *Grands Écrivains* edition favours the retention of *regards*.

15\. **et que . . . sorte**: 'what is it to you that you should put yourself to so much trouble.' Alceste obviously was about to use a clause beginning *de sorte que*. There is some ambiguity, as *pour vous gêner* could be equivalent to *pour que vous vous gêniez* or *pour que cela vous gêne*. The first rendering seems the more probable.

## SCENE III

25\. 11. **point d'affaire**: cf. modern 'nothing doing.'

13\. **que vouloir**: cf. note to page 5, line 7.

16\. **il . . . loisible**: 'you may do just as you please.'

## SCENE IV

26\. 4. **vous prendrez parti**: 'you will make up your mind.'

9\. **du Louvre**: the Louvre was Louis XIV's palace in Paris.

10\. **levé**: see general Introduction, page xi, for a description of this ceremony. Nowadays the form *lever* is used, but both were common in the seventeenth century.

11\. **ridicule achevé**: 'a perfect fool.' Cf. note to page 6, line 30.

12\. **pût**: generic subjunctive; modern sequence of tenses would normally require present subjunctive *puisse* here.

14\. **il se barbouille fort**: *se barbouiller=se rendre ridicule*.

20\. **ne vous déplaise**: 'if you please' (ironical). Cf. note to page 5, line 25.

21\. **chaise**: 'sedan chair.'

24\. **dans . . . goutte**: 'one can never make anything of the conversation which he carries on.'

27\. 7. **sortir du**: 'get away from.'

8\. **commerce**: 'society life.'

27\. 14. **du dernier bien**: 'on the best of terms.'
19\. **à tous coups**: 'at every turn.'
27\. **qu'elle grouille . . . bois**: 'without her budging any more than a block of wood.'
28\. **que . . . Adraste ?**: 'what do you think of Adraste ?'
33\. **fait métier**: 'makes it his occupation.'
35\. **qu'**: *que* here has the sense of *sans que*.
**il se croit**: 'he imagines himself to be.'

28\. 2. **honnêtes**: cf. note to page 4, line 32.
4\. **à qui**: modern French would require *à laquelle* with the omission of the first *à*, or, alternatively, *à qui* would be replaced by *que*.
11\. **en**: nowadays *de lui* following *dites-vous* would be preferred.
15\. **dont**: here equivalent to *ce dont*.
20\. **touche**: 'suits, pleases.'
22\. **n'est . . . esprit**: cf. note to page 15, line 15.
34\. **allons, ferme, poussez**: 'come now, steady, carry on.' Cf. *pousser* on page 29, line 34.

29\. 2. **qu'**: cf. note to page 27, line 35.
15\. **se prendre**: nowadays *s'en prendre à* ('to blame') would be required ; see line 5, above.
35\. **véritable**: *vrai* in modern French.

30\. 1. **se gendarme toujours**: 'is always on the defensive.'
2\. **chagrin**: cf. note to page 2, line 11.
8\. **impertinent**: "qui parle ou agit autrement qu'il ne convient" (Lavigne). Cf. also note to page 9, line 3.
20\. **m'en cacher**: this use of *se cacher de quelque chose* ('to conceal something') is still possible, but it should be noted here that *m'en cacher* is grammatically misrelated with the clause which follows.

31\. 7. **liberté**: 'ease of movement.'
9\. **la malpropre sur soi**: there is some doubt as to what Molière wished to convey by this expression. The *Grands Écrivains* edition suggests that it refers to a woman "peu soucieuse de ses habits, de peu d'élégance et de goût dans sa mise ou sa parure."
18\. **jusqu'aux défauts**: 'the very faults.'
27\. **à moins . . . importunée**: to-day a subjunctive construction with *à moins que* would be preferred. Translate 'unless I note that Madame is inconvenienced.'

31. 30. **couché**: see general Introduction (p. xi), and note to page 26, line 10.

34. **que vous voudrez qui sorte**: 'whom you want to go out.' This type of construction was common in Molière's time, but is considered clumsy to-day. In modern prose *qui sorte* would probably be replaced by an infinitive construction, *e.g.*, *voir sortir*.

## SCENE V

32. 5. **grand'basques plissées**: 'pleated skirts'; *grand* would agree in modern French. Cf. note to page 10, line 3.

6. **avec du dor**: *avec de l'or*. Later editions give *du d'or*. The popular form *dor* is a corruption of *d'or* as in *pièce d'or*. The word is used by the peasant Pierrot in *Don Juan* II. 1.

9. This line is addressed to the *garde*. To prevent duels, which had been formally forbidden by an edict in 1651, a tribunal was established, composed of the marshals of France and presided over by a *doyen*. The latter had a body of *gardes* who carried out his commands. As soon as any quarrel between noblemen came to his notice, he summoned them to appear before him so that a reconciliation might be effected.

## SCENE VI

33. 5. **la voix**: 'judgment.'

22. **par le sangbleu**: 'zounds'; a corruption of *par le sang Dieu*. Cf. note to page 4, line 5.

25. **où**: *là où* in modern French.

# ACT III

## SCENE I

34. 3. **sans t'éblouir les yeux**: 'without deceiving yourself.'

6. **où . . . sujet**: 'where to discover any cause.'

34\. 10. **dont . . . passe:** 'which I am not in an advantageous position to obtain.' The idiom is derived from the term *être en passe* which was used in billiards and the game of 'mall' (according to the Dictionnaire de l'Académie, 1694).

11\. **pour le cœur:** 'as for courage.'

13\. **pousser:** 'pursue.'

**une affaire:** *i.e., une affaire d'honneur.*

15\. **pour de:** 'as for.'

16\. **à:** the preposition is used here to denote purpose.

18\. **bancs:** these seats were placed on the stage itself—a custom which dated from the days of the mystery plays, and which fell into disuse in 1759. It was the fashion in Molière's day for young noblemen to sit on either side of the stage. Their presence there was hardly desirable, as the next two lines indicate.

19\. **faire du fracas:** 'applaud rousingly.'

20\. **endroits:** 'passages.'

**des has:** the interjection *ha* would remain invariable in the plural nowadays. Some editions give *ahs*, and that of 1734 gives the singular *ah*. Lines 17–20 were omitted when the play was performed.

26\. **bien . . . maître:** 'in favour with the king.'

35\. 4. **je . . . humeur:** 'I am neither of the mould nor of the temperament.'

6\. **mal tournés:** *i.e., qui ont mauvaise tournure.* We should nowadays use *mal fait.* Translate 'ungainly.'

**mérites vulgaires:** 'undistinguished people.'

7\. **à brûler:** in modern French, *de* would be used here and before the following infinitives.

**constamment:** used here as the equivalent of *avec constance.*

10\. **suite:** *durée.*

16\. **se faire honneur de:** 'to boast of the conquest of.'

17\. **ce . . . raison:** *il n'est pas raisonnable.*

20\. **être fort bien:** cf. note to page 34, line 26.

25\. **qui:** cf. note to page 16, line 3.

36\. 3. **me dis:** *dis-moi.*

5\. **grande:** the adjective is probably made to follow for the purpose of rhyme, or possibly for emphasis

10\. **qui:** 'if one of us'; usually *qui* in this obsolete construction indicates *si quelqu'un,* but here *si l'un de nous* would make better sense.

36. 12. prétendu: commentators have interpreted this word in a variety of ways, but 'claimant' would seem to be the most likely reading.
15. du bon . . . cœur: preferably *du meilleur de mon cœur* nowadays. Cf. page 49, line 23. Translate 'with all my heart.'

## SCENE III

38. 2. qui: cf. note to page 16, line 3.
5. franche grimace: 'downright hypocrisy,' or possibly 'pretence.'
10. son triste mérite: 'her sorry worth.'
12. tâche à: cf. note to page 8, line 26.
22. à mon gré: 'to my mind.'
23. impertinente: cf. note to page 30, line 8.

## SCENE IV

27. pour: *à cause de*.
30. The 1734 edition gives the following stage direction after this line: "Clitandre et Acaste sortent en riant."

39. 5. aux choses: *dans les choses* would be more usual nowadays.
12. avec ses grands éclats: 'with the scandalous rumours to which it gives rise.'
15. galanterie: *vie galante, i.e.*, fondness for flirtations and a gay life.
16. qu'il . . . fallu: 'than it ought' (pleonastic *ne*).
27. il . . . fasse: 'there is not a single unpleasant story which is not circulated everywhere concerning it.'
28. vos déportements: 'your conduct.' Nowadays the word is used in a bad sense.
29. donner prise aux: 'lay itself open to.'

40. 1. qu'aux mouvements: in modern French we would say *à autre chose qu'aux mouvements*.
6. j'en . . . faveur: 'I wish straightway to acknowledge the service rendered by it.'
20. aux ombres d'indécence: 'at the merest semblance of impropriety.'
21. que . . . innocence: 'which an innocent but ambiguous word may assume.'

40\. 22. **où vous êtes de vous:** 'in which you hold your self.'
31\. **gens:** 'servants.'
33\. **blanc:** cf. note to page 5, line 34.
41\. 6. **vous . . . vôtres:** 'trouble a little more about your own.'
11\. **encor . . . remettre:** 'further, it is better to leave it.' Note inversion after *encore* used in this sense.
16\. Note how in this and the preceding lines Célimène uses Arsinoé's own words and expressions in order the more to confuse and humiliate her. These speeches reveal Molière's dramatic skill and ingeniousness.
17\. **à quoi . . . assujettie:** 'whatever one may lay oneself open to by reprimanding.' Note concord between *on* and *assujettie*. Arsinoé is referring to herself, which explains the agreement: though *on* is generally considered to be a masculine pronoun, adjectives and participles may agree when the use is personal and specific as here.
23\. **traitant de bonne foi:** 'acting in good faith.'
25\. **il . . . vous:** cf. note to page 23, line 28.
26\. **ne:** cf. note to page 23, line 28.
35\. **en prendre le parti:** 'decide to take to it.'
42\. 2. **fâcheuses disgrâces:** Translate freely: 'time's relentless blight.'
8\. **vous . . . terriblement:** 'you make a dreadful fuss about.' Cf. "Elle fait bien sonner ce grand amour de mère" (Corneille, *Rodogune*, line 735).
10\. **un si grand cas:** 'a matter of such importance.' To-day we would say *une si grande affaire*.
12\. **pousser:** 'to provoke.'
14\. **vous déchaîner sur moi:** 'inveighing against me'; *contre* would be more usual here than the *sur* to which Voltaire takes exception.
15\. **vous prendre:** cf. note to page 29, line 15.
16\. **puis-je mais des:** 'can I help.'
24\. **vous faites la vaine:** 'you pride yourself.'
27\. **à voir comme tout roule:** 'when they (*i.e.*, people) see how things go.' Nowadays *comment* would be used. Cf. note to page 4, line 2.
31\. **on ne s'aveugle point:** *on ne se laisse point aveugler.* **défaites:** 'subterfuges.'

42\. 32. **en**: refers to a noun, which has not been stated: 'certain ladies.'

33\. **à**: *pour*.

43\. 5. **d'une si grande gloire**: 'with such (vain) pride.'

6\. **brillants**: 'lustre'; the singular is still used with this meaning; *petits* has the sense of 'insignificant, puny.'

8\. **de traiter**: this infinitive explains *orgueil*; translate 'which makes you treat.'

20\. **arrêter**: *rester*.

26\. **un mot de lettre**: 'a few lines.'

## SCENE V

44\. 5. **charmes**: 'charms' with the meaning of 'magic spells.'

11\. **sur quoi . . . prétendre?**: 'on what grounds could I make any claims on it?'

15\. **qu'on ne fait rien pour moi**: modern French would prefer *de ce qu'on ne fait rien*.

31\. **n'a rien . . . confonde**: 'confuses every issue, confounds everything.'

35\. **la Gazette**: subsequently called *la Gazette de France*, was the first French newspaper. It was founded under Richelieu's patronage in 1631 and ceased to appear in 1914.

45\. 4. **pour peu . . . mines**: 'if you as much as give us the sign that you would contemplate it'; *faire les mines de* to-day appears unusual.

8\. **y**: *à la cour*.

15\. **jouer**: *tromper*.

25\. **essuyer la cervelle de**: 'put up with the (hare-brained) fatuity of.' The figure of speech in which *cervelle=les sottises de gens qui ont la cervelle légère* is called metonymy.

**francs**: cf. note to page 7, line 13.

46\. 7. **toute mon amie**: 'although she is my friend,' *i.e.*, *toute mon amie qu'elle est*. Cf. note to page 16, line 29.

9\. **feintes douceurs**: 'simulated affection.'

11\. **se serait bien passée de**: *aurait bien pu se passer de*, 'might well have abstained from.' Some commentators take this to be equivalent to *aurait bien dû se passer*.

22. **vous fassent foi**: 'should bear you witness.'

23. **donnez-moi . . . chez moi**: gentlemen escorting ladies in the seventeenth century in France offered them the hand, not the arm as at the present time.

## ACT IV

### SCENE I

47. 1. **à manier si dure**: 'so hard to handle.'

6. **ces messieurs**: *i.e.*, *Messieurs les maréchaux*. Cf. note to page 32, line 9.

11. **de travers**: 'amiss.' Nowadays, expressions such as *prendre de travers, entendre de travers* usually=*mal comprendre*.

13. **ce . . . matières**: 'it is not with honour that such matters are concerned'; nowadays when *toucher =concerner*, it more frequently governs the accusative, but the given construction is still used.

14. **en**: *de* in modern French.

15. **de cœur**: cf. page 34, line 11

17. **son train**: *i.e.*, *train de vie*—'way of living.'

19. **je suis son serviteur**: 'no, thank you' (ironical), 'I draw the line there.' "Se dit de quelqu'un quand on n'est pas de son avis, quand on refuse ce qu'il propose, ce qu'il demande" (Littré).

22. **qu'on**: *à moins qu'on*.

**sur peine de**: *sous peine de* is the modern usage.

24. **où**: cf. note to page 10, line 10.

48. 3. **envelopper**: 'wind up.'

5. **en**: cf. note to page 28, line 11.

6. "Voilà sans doute ce que Molière veut que nous pensions d'Alceste. Rousseau aurait bien dû méditer ce couplet d'Éliante" (Lavigne). See Introduction, pages xlvii–xlviii.

13. **de l'humeur**: *i.e.*, *étant de l'humeur*.

21. **aux choses**: *par, d'après les choses* in modern French.

27. **qu'il . . . rien**: *qu'il=quand il*.

34. **je . . . façons**: 'I make no bones about it.'

49. 2. **pour elle s'intéresse:** the meaning of the verb is much stronger than in modern French; cf. "Mon cœur, mon lâche cœur, *s'intéresse* pour lui" (Racine, *Andromaque*, line 1404). Translate 'is deeply interested in it.'

3. **si c'était qu'à moi:** *s'il arrivait qu'à moi.*

7. **d'un autre . . . feux:** 'she should reciprocate the love of someone else.' See note to page 8, line 24; cf. page 70, line 26.

9. **et le refus . . . répugnance:** 'and, in such circumstances, his having been rejected would not cause me to find anything distasteful in it'; *y* refers to *à recevoir ses vœux.* The couplet is elliptical.

17. **tenteraient:** 'would strive to win.'

19. **s'y pourra dérober:** 'can disengage itself from it,' *i.e.,* 'from your favour.'

23. **et:** the co-ordinating conjunction has here the sense of *au contraire.* In seventeenth-century French, *et* was often used where to-day we would employ *car, mais, donc,* and other conjunctions. **du meilleur de mon âme:** cf. page 36, line 15.

## SCENE II

26. **faites-moi raison:** 'avenge me.'

50. 4. **tâche à:** cf. note to page 8, line 26. **se rappeler:** 'collect itself.'

7. **qui:** *qui* here may be either the usual interrogative pronoun or the neuter *qu'est-ce qui.* Cf. note to page 16, line 3.

18. **que l'avoir:** cf. note to page 5, line 7.

20. **produit à:** 'revealed to.' **disgrâce:** 'misfortune.'

30. **ouvrage:** 'task,' *i.e., l'ouvrage de me venger et de me consoler.*

51. 15. **fait force desseins:** 'forms many plans'; to-day *former* would be more usual than *faire.*

19. **un courroux d'un amant:** 'a lover's wrath'; modern usage would require either *un courroux d'amant* or *le courroux d'un amant.*

## SCENE III

52. 13. **témoins**: 'proofs'; in this sense *témoignages* would more often be used in modern French. See also page 53, line 29; page 65, line 8; page 66, line 26.

19. **mon astre me disait**: 'my star told me.' Belief in astrology was common in France during the seventeenth century.

23. **sans dépendance**: 'untrammelled.'

25. **libre à**: now *libre de*.

26. **aussi ne trouverais-je**: 'consequently, I should not find.'

28. **rejetant . . . abord**: 'if you had spurned my love from the very first'; for construction, cf. note to page 4, line 3.

30. **ma flamme applaudie**: although the sense is clear, the expression is faulty: *applaudir* cannot properly be used to qualify *flamme*.

53. 1. **percé**: the participle, although unrelated, obviously refers to Alceste.

16. **mettre à bout**: 'bring to confusion.'

17. **vos traits**: *i.e.*, *traits de plume*, 'your handwriting.'

24. **pour . . . seing**: 'because it bears no signature.' Cf. note to page 7, line 9.

27. **vers moi**: modern French would require *envers* here; *vers moi* would now mean 'towards me' of direction but not of feeling.

29. **témoin**: cf. note to page 52, line 13.

54. 1. **je veux**: 'I am willing.'

3. **vers moi**: cf. note to page 53, line 27.

11. **par quel biais**: 'by what shift.'

**de quel air**: *air* is here rather stronger than *manière*, and approaches *front* in meaning; translate 'with what effrontery.'

15. **ajustez**: 'reconcile.'

18. **d'user . . . empire**: 'to exercise such authority.'

20. **s'emporter**: in view of subsequent *prenez, vous emporter* would be required in modern French for grammatical sequence and accuracy.

32. **faites, prenez parti**: 'go on, make a decision.'

33. **et . . . tête**: 'do not plague me any longer.'

55. 4. **pousse . . . à bout:** 'arouses to the utmost degree.'
5. **fait gloire de:** 'prides herself on.'
8. **généreux:** 'noble.'
12. **ménager:** 'exploit.'
16. **rendez . . . innocent:** 'reveal to me, if you can, the innocence of this letter.'
17. **à . . . mains:** 'to lend you a helping hand'; note the mixed metaphors in this line.
22. **qui:** *ce qui*; cf. note to page 16, line 3.
24. **d'autre côté:** the indefinite article would be used nowadays before *autre*.

56. 1. **en ne s'assurant pas à:** the modern equivalent of *s'assurer à quelque chose* is *se rassurer sur*. Translate 'in not placing his trust in.'
2. **on . . . après:** 'one does not declare, unless after.' It would appear that *ne . . . point que* is not quite the equivalent of the modern *ne . . . que*: "*point* n'est pas un pléonasme; il exprime fortement la négation et *que* prend le sens de *si ce n'est*" (Lavigne).
5. **je veux mal à:** 'I am annoyed at.'
13. **toute abandonnée:** *tout* is now invariable unless it precedes a feminine adjective beginning with a consonant or *h* aspirate. In the seventeenth century it was variable in all cases.
23. **en:** *à* is now found after *réduire* used in this way.
24. **en naissant:** *i.e.*, *à votre naissance*. Cf. note to page 4, line 3.
27. **vous . . . injustice:** 'might make amends to you for the injustice of such a destiny.'
32. **que . . . matière:** 'that you should have occasion.'
33. **plaisamment figuré:** 'amusingly rigged out'; one editor interprets the expression as follows: "c'est-à-dire *avec une plaisante figure* et un *équipage* qui a lieu de surprendre." The following line might well justify such an interpretation.

## SCENE IV

57. 1. **que veut:** *i.e.*, *veut dire*—'what is the meaning of.'
5. **mystères:** 'mysterious matters.'
13. **que d'amusement:** 'what delay.' Cf. Tartuffe: "Le moindre *amusement* vous peut être fatal."

57\. 17. **déloger sans trompette**: 'decamp untrumpeted'; the expression =*partir clandestinement.*

23\. **plier bagage**: 'make off.' Note that Dubois' terminology (*faire retraite, déloger sans trompette, plier bagage*) is of military origin.

29\. **pis qu'un démon**: 'craftier than the devil.'

30\. **de**: *au sujet de.*

31\. **n'y verrait goutte**: 'could make neither head nor tail of it.'

58\. 1. **démêler**: 'to do' (in the sense of 'to be concerned with').

4\. **ensuite**: we should now say *après*. Auger terms this use of *ensuite* "un barbarisme," but it must be remembered that Dubois is speaking.

9\. **comme**: cf. note to page 4, line 2.

17\. **fait un mot**: 'written a note'; *écrire un mot* is common, but *faire* is unusual.

22\. **impertinent au diable**: *i.e., digne d'aller au diable.* Translate 'you blundering wretch'; cf. page 15, line 1.

25\. **qui**: cf. note to page 55, line 22.

27\. **embarras**: 'confusion, perplexing affair.'

29\. **empêcher . . . entretienne**: nowadays *empêcher* used affirmatively as a rule takes *ne* in the dependent *que* clause.

30\. **souffrez**: *permettez.* This use of *souffrir à quelqu'un de faire quelque chose* is now obsolete, though it may still be used with *que* and the subjunctive, *e.g., souffrez que je vous parle.*

## ACT V

### SCENE I

59\. 5. **de ce que je dis**: dependent on *détourner.*

8\. **partie**: 'adversary.'

12\. **succès**: cf. note to page 9, line 27.

18\. **grimace**: cf. note to page 7, line 26.

19\. **tourne**: 'twists, distorts.' The verb is used in the sense of *faire tourner.*

21\. **non content . . . il court**: note the example of anacoluthon here. It is quite clear, however, that *non content* refers to *il* in line 20 and *le fourbe* in line 25.

22. il court: 'there circulates.'
23. de qui: *dont.*

60. 4. j'en use: 'I act, behave.'
11. la gloire: cf. note to page 43, line 5.
17. de ma vie: *jamais.*
18. un peu bien: 'rather too.'
20. vous le faites: 'you represent it.'
21. partie: cf. note to page 59, line 8.
25. lui: *i.e., à lui,* dependent on *nuire.*
27. franc: cf. note to page 7, line 13.
29. en: 'on account of it.'
30. constant: 'definite.'
donné au bruit: *donné dans le bruit, i.e.,* "on ne s'est pas laissé aller à le croire" (Grands Écrivains). Cf. page 5, line 8; page 10, line 23.
34. d'y revenir: 'to reopen it.'

61. 1. m'y tenir: 'abide by it.'
4. à plein: cf. note to page 7, line 14.
16. me vouloir . . . horreurs: we should now rather say *excuser une chose auprès de quelqu'un.*
22. d'autre sorte: cf. note to page 55, line 24.
31. on . . . à: 'we make use of them to.'

62. 7. dispute: 'discussion'; similarly, *disputer* was used for *discúter* in Molière's time.
10. m'en faire foi: cf. note to page 46, line 22.
13. allez-vous-en la voir: cf. note to page 16, line 31.
me laissez: *laissez-moi.*
16. obliger . . . à descendre: here *obliger* does not mean *forcer,* but is the equivalent of *inviter, persuader.*

## SCENE II

19. de votre âme: 'of your affection'; *sur* in modern French.
22. feindre: now obsolete in the sense of 'to hesitate,' as here.
24. vous prétende: cf. note to page 12, line 16.
26. de chez vous: 'from your house'; *de* does not qualify *bannir,* which is used without a preceding preposition.
28. vous . . . vu: 'you whom I have so often seen';

*entendu* would be preferred here in modern French.

64. 5. s'accorde à: *avec* would be used to-day, and indeed *s'accorder avec* is often found in seventeenth-century writings.

6. pareille ardeur: cf. in modern French *pareil exemple*, but use without the article was much commoner in Molière's day than at present.
même: cf. note to page 6, line 20.

8. ne sont plus pour: 'cannot any longer.'

10. je . . . aucunement: nowadays *ne* provides the necessary negation without *pas, point*, etc. Lavigne, however, says that *ne . . . point* here is the real negative and *aucunement* simply an adverb = *d'une manière quelconque* without any negative value.

13. je . . . rien: cf. preceding note.

18. n'y rien prétendre: 'to aspire in no way to her.'

65. 7. rompre en visière: 'to attack openly.' Cf. note to page 6, line 17.

8. témoins: cf. note to page 52, line 13.

14. éclat: 'revelation.'

15. je ne prétends point: 'I have no desire.'

17. amusement: cf. note to page 57, line 13.

23. même chose: cf. note to page 6, line 20.

## SCENE III

29. y paraît concertée: 'seems set upon it'; *y* refers to *à me persécuter*.

30. même chaleur: cf. note to page 6, line 20.

66. 7. et: *car*. Cf. note to page 49, line 23.

10. lâcher la balance: 'have done with prevarication.'

11. poursuivre à: obsolete for *continuer à*.

## SCENE IV

14. sans vous déplaire: 'with your permission.'

19. et: *car*. Cf. note to page 49, line 23.

20. de ma vue: *i.e., de me voir*. Cf. page 24, line 14.

23. à qui: *auquel*.

26. ont démenti: 'have discredited.' Translate the line freely: 'I have discredited the strongest proofs set before my eyes.'
témoins: cf. note to page 52, line 13.

66\. 27. **passant sur:** 'overlooking.'
**discords:** 'disagreements.' Nowadays *discordes* or *désaccords*, but *discord* is still used in poetic and elevated style.

67\. 2. **vous vous prendrez à:** 'you will set about.' To convey this meaning in modern French *s'y prendre pour* would be necessary.

5\. **ces traits:** 'this handwriting.' Cf. note to page 53, line 17.

8\. **à . . . instruire:** 'has served only too well to make you familiar with her writing.'

9\. **de le lire:** *d'être lu, qu'on le lise,* would be required in modern French.

10\. "Vous êtes un étrange homme, *Clitandre,* de . . ." was given in the 1682 and 1734 editions.

14\. **flandrin de vicomte:** 'gawk of a viscount'; *flandrin* as an adjective meant 'Flemish' (*de Flandre*) and, used as a substantive, came to indicate, in a derogatory way, any lanky, awkward person. According to Grimarest, the *vicomte* in question existed in real life, but the account in his *Vie de Molière* is not considered entirely reliable.

17\. **ne saurait me revenir:** 'could not appeal to me.'

18\. **durant:** *pendant.* This preposition normally precedes the noun, but occasionally follows it, *e.g., toute sa vie durant.*

22\. **qui me tint . . . main:** *i.e., qui m'accompagna.* Cf. note to page 46, line 23. It is unlikely that any other meaning is intended here.

23\. **mince:** 'trivial.'
**ce sont de ces mérites:** 'they are those *famous* people.' Cf. note to page 35, line 6.

24\. **qui n'ont que la cape et l'épée:** 'who have but cloak and sword.' According to Lavigne, this expression was originally applied to the younger members of a family, forced to pursue a military career, as the elder brothers received all the inheritance. It is still used to denote an impecunious state, and also, by extension, to describe a person of inferior and superficial merit.
**pour l'homme aux rubans verts:** 'as for the man with the green ribbons,' *i.e.,* Alceste. The ribbons indicate that Alceste was fashionably dressed.

67\. 26. **à vous le dé:** 'it's your turn.' The metaphor is derived from games in which each player in turn throws the dice.

28\. **son chagrin bourru:** 'his churlish ill-humour.'

29\. **l'homme à la veste:** *i.e.*, Oronte. Not only was the vest a new fashion in 1666, but Oronte no doubt attracted special attention by wearing one of exaggerated stylishness.

30\. **voici votre paquet:** 'here is your share.'

31\. **s'est jeté dans le bel esprit:** 'has embarked upon fine wit.' Cf. note to page 15, line 15.

35\. **je vous trouve à dire:** 'I miss you.' Cf. the similar use of *à dire*=' wanting' in *Don Juan* I. 2: "il n'y a plus rien à dire" (=il n'y a plus rien qui nous manque). According to Lavigne, this expression is still used in certain parts of France.

68\. 5. **fait tant le doucereux:** cf. note to page 22, line 16.

10\. **d'en être obsédée:** 'to be importuned by him.'

15\. **belle est la matière:** 'there is very good reason,' or possibly 'the subject is good.'

18\. **du plus haut prix:** the 1682 and 1734 editions give "*de* plus haut prix," which seems preferable since it renders Acaste's annoyance all the more vehement.

24\. **faites un bien:** 'render a service'—now obsolete.

25\. **j'y profite:** 'I thereby win.'

31\. **me sens émouvoir:** here *émouvoir*=*m'émouvoir*.

34\. **monsieur . . . bonheur:** 'this gentleman whom it was your good fortune to attract.'

69\. 6. **prendre sa querelle:** 'take up its cause.'

13\. **créance:** *croyance* here in modern French. *Créance* is still used, however, with a meaning approximating to that of *croyance* in a number of expressions, *e.g.*, *trouver créance*.

16\. **portez-le moins haut:** 'lower your pride.' Cf. page 18, line 11.

25\. The grammatical construction is somewhat loose here. The first *en* probably has the force of *de le faire*, so that *de reprocher* is a second dependent infinitive.

70\. 9. **pousser . . . bout:** 'carry to the utmost limit, extremity.'

11\. **il est . . . homme:** 'there is always some human weakness.'

70\. 14. couvrirai: 'shall conceal, excuse'; *me* is probably ethic dative.

16\. veuille . . . mains: 'is willing to contribute its help.' This line provides a striking example of mixed metaphors.

26\. s'il faut: 'if it should be.' See also page 8, line 24; page 49, line 7.

32\. prendre un dessein: nowadays *concevoir* or *former un dessein* is used. *Se proposer un dessein* (page 71, line 34) is also rare.

71\. 3. vous n'êtes point . . . pour trouver: 'you cannot find, you are not of a nature to find.' Cf. page 5, line 9.

5\. sensible: 'deeply felt.'

17\. le rebut . . . pas: Translate freely: 'the affection spurned by a heart which had not your worth.'

21\. sans trop m'inquiéter: *sans que je m'inquiète trop*. Cf. page 13, line 27? and note.

22\. pourrait: 'might.'

25\. y: *pour cela, i.e.*, 'for that honour.'

34\. dessein . . . se propose: cf. note to page 70, line 32.